UNITY LIBRARY 8 ARCHIVES
Preaching without notes
BV 4211 .M14

0 0051 0035750 1

SO-AEC-268

PREACHING WITHOUT NOTES

PREACHING
WITHOUT NOTES

By

CLARENCE EDWARD MACARTNEY

MINISTER, FIRST PRESBYTERIAN CHURCH
PITTSBURGH, PENNSYLVANIA

BAKER BOOK HOUSE
Grand Rapids, Michigan

UNITY SCHOOL LIBRARY
UNITY VILLAGE, MISSOURI 64065

Copyright 1946 by Stone & Pierce
Paperback edition issued 1976 by
Baker Book House Company
ISBN: 0-8010-5992-5
First printing, July 1976

PHOTOLITHOPRINTED BY CUSHING - MALLOY, INC.
ANN ARBOR, MICHIGAN, UNITED STATES OF AMERICA
1 9 7 6

Introduction

Clarence Edward Macartney (1879-1957)
PREACHING WITHOUT NOTES

I have heard this preacher in his pulpit masterfully proclaiming the eternal Gospel. He served churches in Paterson, N. J., Philadelphia, and for twenty-seven years pastored the First Presbyterian Church, Pittsburgh. What is written in these six exciting chapters is a digest of his strongly held convictions concerning the Christian ministry. Only one chapter bears the theme of the book, but the background for the delivery of the sermon or the address does not come easily, hence Dr. Macartney stresses the preparation of the man and his message.

Dr. Macartney came of Covenanting stock. Puritan in spirit, he evidenced the shepherd-heart as he "pastored" his people, visiting their homes, caring for the needy, toiling daily in preparation for five preaching-teaching messages each week. He made wise use of illustrations culled from his experiences and travel as well as wide reading. He possessed natural gifts of speech and debate which led to a disciplined and logical order in preaching. His library was comprehensive and yet selective in its major works for reference and afforded mental and spiritual stimulus.

The Bible was the seminal basis of all his preaching. Bible characters, events, sayings, his whole library was harnessed to one end — to make God in Christ known in the power of the Holy Spirit to those who listened in church or by radio. Macartney believed in "series of sermons" and his strong biographical sermons were outstanding. His best known sermon was "Come Before Winter," given first at the Arch Street Presbyterian Church, Philadelphia, and then by request repeated each year there and at Pittsburgh until it was delivered some forty times!

More topical than expository in treatment, the sermons were carefully exegeted from Scripture texts. The evangelical note sounded forth with concern and compassion. The printed page cannot convey the light in the eye, the glow of the cheek, the gesture of the hand, the attitude of the body, the resonant music of the voice . . . the thunder and the lightning are gone. But the welcome reissue of this volume will go far to introduce a new generation to a master preacher and his meticulous and thorough preparation for preaching — and that without notes! Pastors and students who take this as a summons to new adventures in ministry will find in these six chapters a post-graduate course in Practical Theology.

RALPH G. TURNBULL

FOREWORD

In common with most preachers, I would rather preach than talk about preaching—that is, talk about the methods and plans of preaching. Nevertheless, those who stand in the pulpit from Sunday to Sunday may derive benefit from the exchange of experience in preaching and its preparation. In this book that is what I have tried to do. I have drawn upon the experience of forty-one years in the pulpit. On most of the themes dealt with in these chapters I have spoken to the students of many theological seminaries, and also before gatherings and conferences of ministers. Four of the chapters, in substance, were delivered at the Princeton Institute of Theology, 1944. The response and interest aroused on these occasions suggest that a record of these addresses may be welcomed by ministers and theological students who did not hear them.

In the printed page I have retained the personal note of the spoken addresses, since this book is not designed to be a textbook in homiletics. It is the account of my own experience in study and preparation for the pulpit, and in preaching.

CLARENCE EDWARD MACARTNEY

5

CONTENTS

I

THE RECALL TO GOSPEL PREACHING

VERY EARLY IN MY MINISTRY I CHANCED TO READ IN the *British Weekly,* one of the most widely read religious journals, an article by the editor, Sir William Robertson Nicoll, in which he related his experiences in worshiping in churches in the south of England during a period of convalescence after a long illness. He spoke of the sober order and dignity of the services, and how the preachers were well-educated and sincere men who delivered thoughtful and carefully prepared sermons. But at the end of the article he said: "Not one of them would have converted a titmouse!"

That sentence of indictment has often come back to me in the many years which have passed since I read that article—"Not one of them would have converted a titmouse!" Across how many of our sermons, if the truth were told, would that indictment have to be written! There are, it is true, sermons for comfort and instruction, for condemnation, for special occasions. Nevertheless, the great aim and purpose of the sermon is to convert the sinner to the will of God in Christ. Our commission is still that which was given by our Lord himself to Paul: "To open their eyes, and to turn them from darkness to light, and from the power of Satan unto God, that they may receive forgiveness of sins, and inheritance among them which are sanctified by faith." Nothing less than that is the great objective of the preacher, as given to him by the Lord of Glory himself. It is this aim and purpose which makes the preacher's office the grandest upon earth and bestows upon him honors and laurels incorruptible, undefiled, and that fade not away, compared with which the laurels of a Caesar or a Napoleon are but withered weeds. That is why the true pulpit

> Must stand acknowledg'd, while the world shall stand,
> The most important and effectual guard,
> Support, and ornament of Virtue's cause.
> There stands the messenger of truth : there stands
> The legate of the skies—His theme divine,
> His office sacred, his credentials clear.
> By him the violated law speaks out
> Its thunders; and by him, in strains as sweet
> As angels use, the Gospel whispers peace.[1]

As we direct our thought to gospel, or, literally, evangelical, preaching—that is, preaching *according to the gospel*—we shall consider, first, the necessity of evangelical preaching; second, some of the conditions of successful evangelical preaching; and, third, its exceeding great reward.

The title of this chapter, "The Recall to Gospel Preaching," assumes, of course, that there has been in many places a departure from gospel preaching. I do not think it is necessary to argue this proposition. It

[1] Cowper, *The Task*, Book II.

is a confession freely made in many places and by men of different communions. When, for example, one can go through newspaper excerpts of forty sermons preached on a Sunday in metropolitan pulpits and find only one mention of sin, the inevitable conclusion must be that where the need for the gospel was not declared, the gospel itself, the good tidings of salvation, was not spoken.

Recently I made an analysis of sermons which appeared in one of the most widely read pulpit magazines. Here are some of the leading ideas in these sermons: "What shall I do then with Jesus which is called Christ?" (Matt. 27:22.) An excellent setting forth of the ethical side of Christianity, but with a discounting of creed and dogma, and a fling at the Council of Nicaea for proclaiming that Jesus is God, but not caring whether a man hated his brother or not, so long as he believed that dogma. "The Use of Common Things in Life," based on "What is that in thine hand?" (Exod. 4:2.) What Newton learned from an apple and Watt from a teakettle, what David did with his sling and what Galileo saw through a bit of glass. "The Meaning of Forgiveness," based on "There is forgiveness with thee, that thou mayest be feared." (Ps. 130:4.) The supreme proof of the goodness of God is to be found in the life and death of Christ. Man must answer God's forgiveness by forgiving his brother. The power of forgiveness in ethical and social life. Then a sermon based on "All things work together for good." (Rom. 8:22.) This has an interesting and helpful illustration taken

11

from the boll weevil, showing how its devastations led men in the South to produce something else besides cotton.

A great many of the sermons of the day deal with Christian truth as applied to international affairs. For some reason that seems much more interesting to some preachers than Christian truth applied to the individual soul—which certainly is where Christ put the emphasis. I think it can be said that such sermons as I have outlined above are characteristic of much of the preaching of our day. There is much that is suggestive and helpful and stimulating, but it would have to be said of them what Nicoll said of the sermons to which he listened in the south of England: "Not one of them would have converted a titmouse!"

THE NECESSITY OF EVANGELICAL PREACHING

The Apostle Paul was fond of what we might describe as the accumulating climax, or the pyramidical sentence. He delighted in placing one great proposition and truth upon another, until from one grand and solid base he reached an exalted and sublime apex. An example is his famous passage in the eighth chapter of Romans, where he ascends the steps of the pyramid from the eternal predestination of God to the final state of glory of the redeemed soul: "For whom he did foreknow, he also did predestinate to be conformed to the image of his Son, that he might be the firstborn among many brethren. Moreover whom he did predestinate, them he also called: and whom he called, them he also justified: and whom he justified, them he also glorified."

But in another passage—the tenth chapter of Romans —the apostle, instead of ascending the steps of the pyramid, descends its steps, from the salvation of the soul, and the glory of that salvation, at the summit, down to the soul's first hearing of the gospel: "If thou shalt confess with thy mouth the Lord Jesus, and shalt believe in thine heart that God hath raised him from the dead, thou shalt be saved. For with the heart man believeth unto righteousness; and with the mouth confession is made unto salvation. . . . For whosoever shall call upon the name of the Lord shall be saved. How then shall they call on him in whom they have not believed? and how shall they believe in him of whom they have not heard? and how shall they hear without a preacher? and how shall they preach, except they be sent? as it is written, How beautiful are the feet of them that preach the gospel of peace, and bring glad tidings of good things!"

There are three great facts declared in this memorable passage: that men are saved by faith in Christ Jesus, that they cannot have that faith in Christ until they hear of it, and that they cannot hear without a preacher. The necessity for the preacher, the content of his message, and the reward of the preacher are all beautifully illustrated in the story of Philip and the treasurer of Queen Candace. When Philip ascended the Ethiopian's chariot, he found him reading from the fifty-third chapter of Isaiah, how "he was led as a sheep to the slaughter; and like a lamb dumb before his shearer, so opened he not his mouth: in his humiliation his judgment was

13

taken away: and who shall declare his generation? for his life is taken from the earth." But the Ethiopian did not know what that meant and asked Philip, "Of whom speaketh the prophet this? of himself, or of some other man?" Then Philip began with the same scripture and preached unto him Jesus, until the Ethiopian believed, confessed his belief, saying, "I believe that Jesus Christ is the Son of God," and was baptized. There you have the necessity for the preacher; the preacher's message, Christ and him crucified; and the objective of the preacher, the conversion and the salvation of the soul.

The preaching of the gospel is necessary, not only because men must hear it to be saved, but because it is the only gospel by which men can be saved. It is one thing to preach the gospel as *a* way or a very good way, or even the best way, and another thing to preach it as the *only* way. The gospel is both universal and exclusive—universal in that it is offered to all men, exclusive in that it declares that it is the only way of salvation. Christ did not say that he was *a* way, but that he was *the* way, *the* truth, and *the* life. He did not say that he was *a* door, but that he was *the* door, and that whoever tried to come into the sheepfold some other way, the same was a thief and a robber. Peter declared to the rulers and elders and scribes and the people at Jerusalem, "Neither is there salvation in any other: for there is none other name under heaven given among men whereby we must be saved."

From the very beginning, immense pressure was exerted to tone down the gospel and make it something else than an exclusive gospel, to take out of it what Dr. Thomas Chalmers liked to describe as "the grand particularities" of the gospel. It is evident that Paul felt that pressure to tone down the gospel in Galatia. If he would only yield in one thing, and agree with the Judaizers that not only faith in Christ, but also the old Jewish rites were necessary to salvation, then his troubles and his persecutions would be over. "Then," as he put it, "is the offence of the cross ceased." And that is the offense of the cross—its exclusiveness. Perhaps Paul felt that pressure to abandon the exclusiveness of the gospel when he went down from Athens to Corinth. At all events, his experience in preaching to the philosophers on Mars' Hill had filled him with a new humility and with the determination to preach in a single-minded way the truths of redemption; for he says in his letter to the church at Corinth: "I, brethren, when I came to you, came not with excellency of speech or of wisdom, declaring unto you the testimony of God. For I determined not to know anything among you, save Jesus Christ, and him crucified. And I was with you in weakness, and in fear, and in much trembling." The preacher of today must have a similar determination if he is to resist successfully the pressure of the world against the exclusiveness of the gospel.

Too many of our sermons lack that which is distinctively Christian. At the close of a church service a man spoke to the preacher about his sermon and concluded, "There was one thing lacking." "What was that?" asked the preacher. The man answered, "I am a

15

Jew. I have only recently been born again. Up to that time I attended the synagogue. There was really nothing in your sermon that I could not have heard in the synagogue, nothing that a Jewish rabbi might not have preached." In after years the preacher confessed, "That was the greatest lesson in homiletics I was ever taught."

I recently read an address by the able and gifted chaplain of one of the most famous of our universities, in which he dwelt upon the catholicity of his chapel pulpit. I noted his statement that those who listened to the men who preached there—Roman Catholics, Protestants, Jews, Unitarians, Friends, and humanitarians—were struck with the fact that there was little difference in their messages, and that no one could know from the sermon to what family of faith the preacher belonged. He cited this as a great tribute to the pulpit of that chapel. And yet one wonders what Peter or Paul or John would have thought, if they had chanced to come into the chapel on those Sabbaths and listened to those sermons. Of all of those sermons it might be said what Dr. McCosh said of the sermons of the minister who baptized him: "They are gracefully written in short and well-constructed sentences, and they have fine sentiment, but they do not contain one sentence of gospel truth, that is, of Jesus set forth as the Redeemer of sinners." When the pulpit strikes no distinctively Christian note, then the next thing is that almost any opinion may be heard from the pulpit. So Bishop Gore in his book *Belief in God* writes: "There is nothing today which is not both affirmed and denied in Christian pulpits."

An interesting example of the pressure to tone down the exclusiveness of the gospel is found in A. J. Cronin's popular novel *The Keys of the Kingdom*. In that book the author sketches what is in many ways an admirable and lovable character, Father Chisholm. But he also states, although in somewhat extreme form, the creed of those who have abandoned the exclusiveness of the gospel. The nun, Mother Maria-Veronica, is troubled by the fact that the amiable Dr. Tulloch, who ministered to the Chinese in the plague, was an atheist, and died one. But Father Chisholm tells her: "There is one thing we most of us forget. Christ taught it. The Church teaches it—though you wouldn't think so to hear a great many of us today. No one in good faith can ever be lost. No one. Buddhists, Mohammedans, Taoists—the blackest cannibals who ever devoured a missionary—if they are sincere according to their own lights, they will be saved. That is the splendid mercy of God. So why shouldn't He enjoy confronting a decent agnostic at the Judgment Seat with a twinkle in his eye: 'I'm here, you see, in spite of all they brought you up to believe. Enter the Kingdom which you honestly denied.'"

That passage has been read—and no doubt admired— by multitudes of Christian people. But it is wholly contrary to the gospel, and would rob every minister of his commission. It would reduce the gospel to sincerity in whatever a man does or whatever a man believes, however good or bad, false or true, it might be. If this is the gospel, then we have no message to proclaim, and Paul must rewrite that passage, "Whosoever shall call upon the name of the Lord shall be saved. How then shall they call on him in whom they have not believed? and how shall they believe in him of whom they have not heard? and how shall they hear without a preacher?"

THE CONDITIONS FOR SUCCESSFUL GOSPEL PREACHING

One of the conditions for successful gospel preaching is a concern for and desire for the salvation of souls. The prophet said, "As soon as Zion travailed, she brought forth her children." When the Church "travails"—is moved with compassion, as Christ was, over a lost world—then the Church will bring forth her children. Here the preacher appears, not as a chaplain of a little group of people, not as a petty organizer, or executive of an institution, but as a seeker after souls. This concern for men without Christ, living without God and without hope, depends, of course, upon what I have just stated—the exclusiveness of the gospel, and the necessity of its being preached.

Whitefield used to pray over and over again, toward the end of his Spirit-filled and God-owned ministry, "Lord, give me a warm heart!" But we cannot have warm hearts to preach the gospel if we feel that it makes no difference whether men hear the gospel or not, or, if they have heard it, whether they believe it or not. Phillips Brooks used to say, "The heart of the preacher ought to kindle at the sight of a man." As Frederic W. H. Myers put it in his magnificent poem, perhaps the greatest tribute in print to the Apostle Paul:

Only like souls I see the folk thereunder,
Bound who should conquer, slaves who should be
 kings,—
Hearing their one hope with an empty wonder,
Sadly contented in a show of things ;—
Then with a rush the intolerable craving
Shivers throughout me like a trumpet call,—
Oh, to save these! to perish for their saving,
Die for their life, be offered for them all!

A second condition for successful evangelical preaching is the presentation of the cardinal doctrines and
truths of the Christian faith. It is idle to talk of evangelistic sermons, or evangelistic campaigns, if the evangel
itself is left out. The great doctrines concerning the soul,
sin, the person of Christ, the atonement, regeneration,
and salvation, comprise the gospel message, and there
can be no true gospel preaching without them. For a
long period the Church declared a moratorium on the
preaching of theology. It was either completely ignored
or supplanted by a false theology. Now the Church reaps
the dividends in abandoned evening services and prayer-
less prayer meetings, in the dwindling number of those
who are added daily to the Church of them that shall
be saved, and in the increase in worldly living, even
among faithful members of the Church.

When it comes to the content of the preacher's message, we have that from our Lord himself, as related
in the words that Peter spoke to the centurion Cornelius.
These words tell what our Lord after his resurrection
commanded the apostles to preach: "And he commanded

19

us to preach unto the people, and to testify that it is he which was ordained of God to be the Judge of quick and dead. To him give all the prophets witness, that through his name whosoever believeth in him shall receive remission of sins."

For these great facts of the gospel there can be no substitute. A young preacher once went to David Swing, the poet-preacher of Chicago, then at the zenith of his fame and popularity, and himself charged with having departed from the true message of the gospel, and asked him what he could do to hold a congregation on Sunday. Said the young preacher, "I have tried history, biography, literature, poetry, book reviews, politics, but the people won't come. What shall I do?" Swing responded, "Suppose now you try the gospel!"

Among the great doctrines which we must emphasize is the doctrine of the Holy Spirit. Perhaps the most striking change in preaching in the last thirty years is the omission of the Holy Spirit from sermons. If we are to have true evangelical preaching, there must be the recognition of, the honoring of, and the invocation of the Holy Spirit. This is his dispensation and it is his message we proclaim. Only the Holy Spirit can bring souls to repentance toward God and faith in the Lord Jesus Christ. Without his potent aid, without the recognition of his presence and power, we can do nothing. It is only by the Holy Spirit that the soul can say that Christ is God and that in the Cross of Christ there is eternal salvation. Let us pray that God will answer us by fire, and that by his Holy Spirit he will send fire on the earth, that fire of the Spirit which brings **purity,** light, warmth, and power.

A third condition for successful evangelical preaching is prayer. In a sense every earnest, evangelical sermon, calling men to repentance and faith, is prayer in its sublimest form. But in addition there must be prayer before the sermon is preached and after it is preached. Prayer prepares the ground for the seed and nurtures the seed after it has been planted.

The greatest religious movement in the history of America was the Great Revival of the first decade of the nineteenth century, the revival that left us the prayer meeting, the Bible class, the theological seminaries, the Sunday school, the crusade against slavery, the crusade against strong drink, the great missionary enterprise, and a thousand blessings amid which the Church still does its work. That revival sprang up in one of the darkest hours in the nation's history, when James McCready and a few God-fearing men, in the wilderness of Kentucky, made their Covenant with God, in which they bound themselves to meet together every Saturday night "at the set of the sun," and spend a half hour asking God to revive his work and to save souls "in Logan County and throughout the world."

THE JOYS AND REWARDS OF EVANGELICAL PREACHING

One of the rewards of evangelical preaching is the tonic which such preaching supplies for the minister's own life. If the life within the minister's own heart is not right, it will be natural and easy for him to avoid

21

and omit the great searching truths of the gospel. Evangelical preaching reacts upon his own life. It makes him realize how a certain amount of the doubt in the mind of the hearer and of his resistance to the truth may be associated with the life of the preacher himself. Thus it makes him more thoughtful and careful in his own manner of life, more earnest to avoid the snares of levity, worldliness, sloth, selfishness, and lack of love.

Another joy and reward of evangelical preaching is the eloquence and unction that it gives to the preacher himself. The highest eloquence is born of earnestness. You have all noted that. An ignorant laborer or an uneducated woman under the stress of emotion becomes truly eloquent. He is eloquent because he is in dead earnest. In *Confessions of an English Opium-Eater* Thomas De Quincey describes the preaching of one of his four guardians, who was his tutor and also curate of a church in Manchester. De Quincey was compelled not only to listen to his preaching but to reproduce a miniature of the sermon on Monday morning. "As a preacher," he wrote, "Mr. H. was sincere, but not earnest." At first that struck me as strange—"sincere, but not earnest." How could a man be sincere without being earnest? But light was thrown on that by what followed:

He was a good and conscientious man; and he made a high valuation of the pulpit as an organ of civilisation for co-operating with books; but it was impossible for any man, starting from the low ground of themes so unim-

22

passioned and so desultory as the benefits of industry, the danger from bad companions, the importance of setting a good example, or the value of perseverance—to pump up any persistent stream of earnestness either in himself or in his auditors.

A preacher can be sincere on the low ground of prudential ethics and morals, but he becomes earnest only when he seeks the salvation of the souls of his hearers. In this connection, and in that same comment on the preacher of his school days, De Quincey says:

By mere accident, I one day heard quoted a couplet which seemed to me sublime. It described a preacher such as sometimes arises in difficult times, or in fermenting times, a son of thunder, that looks all enemies in the face, and volunteers a defiance even when it would have been easy to evade it. The lines were written by Richard Baxter. ... As a pulpit orator, he was perhaps the Whitfield of the seventeenth century—the *Leuconomos* of Cowper. And thus it is that he describes the impassioned character of his own preaching—

"I preached as never sure to preach again;

[Even *that* was telling; but then followed this thunder-*peal*]

And as a dying man to dying men."

This couplet, which seemed to me equally for weight and for splendor like molten gold, laid bare another aspect of the Catholic church; revealed it as a Church militant and crusading.

Evangelical preaching rewards the preacher with power and eloquence because it makes him realize that he is preaching against time, and he therefore seeks to bring men to an immediate decision for Christ. "How long have you been a Christian?" asked a minister of a woman at the foot of the pulpit stairs after he had concluded an earnest evangelical sermon. "Just now," she answered to his surprise. "I became a Christian while you were preaching there in the pulpit." And why not?

On Sunday night, October 8, 1871, Moody preached to the largest congregation that he had yet addressed in Chicago. His text was, "What shall I do then with Jesus which is called Christ?" At the close of the sermon he said, "I wish you would take this text home with you and turn it over in your minds during the week, and next Sabbath we will come to Calvary and the Cross, and we will decide what to do with Jesus of Nazareth."

Then Sankey began to sing the hymn:

> Today the Saviour calls;
> For refuge fly;
> The storm of justice falls,
> And death is nigh.

But the hymn was never finished, for while Sankey was singing, there came the rush and roar of fire engines on the street outside, and before morning Chicago lay in ashes. To his dying day Moody regretted that he had told that congregation to come next Sabbath and decide what to do with Jesus. "I have never dared," he said, "to give an audience a week to think of their salvation

24

since. If they were lost they might rise up in judgment against me. I have never seen that congregation since. I never will meet those people again until I meet them in another world. But I want to tell you of one lesson that I learned that night, which I have never forgotten, and that is, when I preach, to press Christ upon the people, then and there, and try to bring them to a decision on the spot. I would rather have that right hand cut off than give an audience now a week to decide what to do with Jesus."

Another reward of evangelical preaching is that it gives joy to the people. Sometimes the minister is tempted to say to himself: "Why preach of sin and atonement and redemption and these great truths of the gospel when practically everyone to whom I preach is already a Christian?" But we must not yield to that temptation. They too have their hearts warmed by such preaching. What are the sermons which have made the deepest impressions? Are they not those very sermons which called men to repentance toward God and faith in the Lord Jesus Christ? A preacher would do well to remember St. Bernard. "Yesterday," he said, "I preached myself, and the scholars came up and praised me. Today, I preached Christ, and the sinners came up and thanked me." They who know the way of life best, like best to hear it. How true are those lines of the old hymn:

> I love to tell the story,
>   For those who know it best

Seem hungering and thirsting
To hear it, like the rest.

Finally, evangelical preaching brings the unspeakable reward and joy of saving souls. It is related of a distinguished British preacher of a generation ago that late one night he was summoned from his manse to minister to a dying woman. He had never stressed the great truths of the gospel, and as he sat beside this poor woman in her miserable tenement, he began to talk to her about courage and strength and vision, and all that vague miscellany of modernist preaching. But the woman, after listening a little with a dazed look, lifted her hand and said, "That's all very good and true; but it's no' for the likes o' me. I am just a poor lost sinner, and I want you to tell me how to get into the Kingdom." Then the preacher turned back to the great story of God's love, and how he saves sinners through faith in the crucified Son of God. Relating his experience afterward to some of his fellow ministers, he said, "I got her in; and what is more, I got myself in too!" The preacher's soul is just as infinitely valuable as the soul of any other person, and, like the soul of every other man, the preacher's soul can be saved only through faith in the crucified Son of God. That was the advice—to take heed to his way of life, and to preach the true Christian doctrine—that the greatest of preachers gave to a young minister at Ephesus ages ago: "For in doing this thou shalt *both save thyself, and them that hear thee.*"

CONCLUSION

This is the ever-new, and yet the old gospel, as necessary today as it was when first proclaimed. To that gospel the Church must be recalled. It must advance or retreat, evangelize or die—there is no other alternative. Evangelical preaching is the answer for all our church problems. It is the solvent of all heresies; and the drier and stonier the soil, the more solemn is the duty and responsibility of the preacher to sow the seed of the gospel.

Years ago I had to wait for a train several hours in the old French city of Dijon. To pass the time, I wandered into the ancient cathedral. What I remember now about it—and what spoke to me impressively that day as a young preacher—is the figure of a sculptured angel in the carved pulpit. In his left hand the angel holds a tablet, in his right hand a pen. His head is lifted up, waiting to catch what the preacher will say, that he may write it down. It was evidently the artist's purpose to express in that sculptured angel the responsibility of the preacher. If it is true of all men that we shall give an account of our words—Christ said, "By thy words thou shalt be justified"—then how solemnly true that is of the preacher!

In the northwest tower of St. Paul's Cathedral, London, hangs the ponderous bell known as "Great Paul." The bell bears this inscription from the Vulgate: "Væ mihi si non evangelisavero"—"Woe to me, if I preach not the gospel!" When the apostle spoke these words he

27

meant that he deserved no words of praise for preaching the gospel as he had preached it, because the burden of the gospel was upon him, and had he not preached the gospel that had been given unto him, he would have been worthy of condemnation and the judgment of God. Where ministers feel that they are under the great compulsion, then there will be no question as to the preaching of the gospel, and no turning aside from its grand particularities. There are sacred trusts in life which are committed to men: the trust of a child in its parents, of a mother in her son, of a wife in her husband, of a friend in a friend, of a nation in its soldiers. But none of these can compare with that most sacred and beautiful trust which Christ reposes in those who stand before the world as his ministers. When we step into our pulpit, we go as men who have been trusted of God to declare the glorious gospel of the blessed God.

I wonder if you have ever been in the Highlands of Scotland? The shepherds are a wonderful folk, in some respects the most wonderful folk in the world. In one of those Highland villages there was a shepherd who had a little daughter. He would take her with him when he went out over the moors to tend and fold the sheep. Most of all the daughter liked to hear her father call the sheep with the shepherd's call, sounding free and beautiful, down the wind, over the moors.

By and by the little girl became a beautiful young woman and went off to the great city, Edinburgh or Glasgow, to take a post. At first her letters came regularly every week. Then the intervals between them grew longer, and finally they ceased altogether. There were rumors, too, in the village, that the shepherd's daughter had been seen in gay company and in questionable places. One day a lad from the village who knew her well saw her in the city and spoke to her, but she pretended that she had never seen him before. When the shepherd heard this, he gathered a few things together, and, clad in his shepherd's smock, with his plaid wrapped around his shoulders and his staff in his hand, set out for the city to seek and find his lost daughter.

Day after day he sought her, on the avenues, and in the slums and closes of the city, but in vain. Then he remembered how his daughter loved to hear him give the shepherd's call. Again he set out on his quest of sorrow and love, this time sounding, loud and free, the shepherd's call. Passers-by turned with astonishment to look on the shepherd in his smock and with his staff as he went up and down the streets sounding the shepherd's call. At length in a house on one of the degraded streets of the city his daughter, sitting in a room with her gay companions, suddenly looked up with astonishment in her face. There was no doubt about it! It was her father's voice! The shepherd's call! Flinging wide the door, she rushed out upon the street. There was her father, who took her in his arms and carried her with him to the Highland home, and there loved her back to decency and to God.

The shepherd's call! What preacher knows how much more time he will have to preach the everlasting gospel? Who knows how many more sermons he shall preach?

If you had only one sermon, would you not want it to be a sermon that would echo the Shepherd's call—a sermon that would call the sinner back to his Father's home?

II

THE PREACHER AND HIS ILLUSTRATIONS

IN RUSSIAN CAUCASIA ONE CAN SEE STRANGE-LOOK-ing houses. They are built like a tower, solid, substantial, and lofty, but without a window. In California I have seen a hilltop house constructed almost entirely of glass. The Russian house and the Californian house represent two extremes in architecture—and also two extremes in styles of preaching. There are sermons which are solid, substantial, and orderly, but which have no window of illustration. Then there are sermons which consist almost entirely of illustrations and lack the solid substance of truth. In between these extremes lies the golden mean of preaching. One of the distinguished professors of theology at Princeton a generation ago used to say that a sermon should have no illustrations whatever. Now and then I heard him preach one of his long sermons in the chapel. It was a high order of discourse so far as an exposition of biblical doctrines was concerned, but it tired the mind to listen to the end, for there was not a single relieving flash of illustration. Certainly Christ would not agree with this distinguished professor, for he continually appealed to eye gate, and "without a parable spake he not unto them."

The purpose of illustration is not merely to make the truth clear, but to heighten its nobility and glory. To this day I can remember an absurd illustration used by one of my seminary classmates in his trial sermon when we were licensed by the Presbytery of Philadelphia. He was preaching on that great text about the Church, "Fair as the moon, clear as the sun, and terrible as an army with banners." (Song of Sol. 6:10.) Just what it had to do with his theme I do not recall, but he likened some process to the time it would take for a rat to eat his way through a cheese! This absurd illustration stuck in the minds of the listeners, while they forgot anything worthy he may have said of the Church and its glory. Yet the fact that I remember that one example shows how an illustration stays in the mind of the hearer.

When I was a junior at college, I heard T. de Witt Talmage preach. I can still see him as he stood there, well back on the platform at a lakeside Chautauqua. His form was stalwart, his features clear-cut, his voice strong, somewhat rough yet appealing. He stood there with closed eyes, and for an introduction to his sermon he described a man driving over the Illinois prairie in a buckboard, the crimson and golden flowers brushing the horses' bellies. At the end of this description he opened his eyes, sprang forward to the front of the platform, and with a mighty voice announced his theme and text.

There is no question that a well-done illustration remains in the mind of the hearer after all else is forgotten. Beecher used to say that if the illustrations of a sermon were changed, a preacher could repeat any sermon he had preached six months before and no one would recognize it. A minister once tried this experiment. Some months after he had preached a sermon he asked twenty persons to write down what they could remember. Only one or two remembered the outline or other features, but nearly everyone remembered the closing illustration. Thomas Guthrie, the great Scottish pictorial preacher, got his suggestion for that kind of preaching from the answers he received from the children whom it was his custom to examine on the Sabbath evening regarding his morning sermon. He discovered that what the children remembered was some story or illustration he had used. This convinced him that what was good for children was good for adults, and started him on his great career as a pictorial preacher.

When Abraham Lincoln made his trip to the east in 1860, he spoke at New Haven. The professor of rhetoric at Yale heard him and, greatly taken with his manner of speech, went to hear him again at Hartford. Lincoln asked what it was in his style of speaking that so interested a specialist in rhetoric. The professor answered, "The clearness of your statement, the unanswerable style of your reasoning, and especially your illustrations, which were romance and pathos and fun and logic all welded together."

One of the illustrations which appealed to the professor was the following, used by Lincoln to show how

the slaveholder's property rights influenced his mind
and made him think that slavery was right:

The Dissenting minister who argued some theological
point with one of the Established Church was met by the
reply, "I can't see it so." He opened the Bible and pointed
him to a passage, but the orthodox minister replied, "I
can't see it so." Then he showed him a single word. "Can
you see that?" "Yes, I see it," was the reply. The Dis-
senter laid a guinea over the word and asked, "Do you see
it now?" So here. Whether the owners of this species
of property do really see it as it is, it is not for me to say;
but if they do, they see it as through two billions of dol-
lars, and that is a pretty thick coating.[1]

There can be no doubt about the effectiveness of the
right illustration.

> Truth in closest words shall fail,
> When truth embodied in a tale
> Shall enter in at lowly doors.

God himself is the great Illustrator. When he gave
the world redemption, he gave it not in abstract truth
but in the person of a Redeemer—"The Word was
made flesh, and dwelt among us."

SOURCES OF ILLUSTRATION

The Bible.—There is an old Jewish legend that one
night when David was sleeping on the roof of his pal-

[1] The Dissenting minister was the celebrated Robert Hall, and
the word he covered with the guinea was "God."

ace with his harp hanging near him, the wind from Olivet blew softly across the chords, awakening sweet music. Hearing it, David arose from his bed and composed the Psalms to the music of the harp. The legend embodies the truth that the Bible makes music on all the chords that God has hung in the human heart.

The greatest of all illustrations are the parables and stories of the Bible, particularly those of the Old Testament. The parables of the Old Testament, not nearly so well known as those of the New Testament, afford the preacher not only a fertile field for illustration of truth, but also a great lesson in the use of illustrations. For example, we might cite Ezekiel's chambers of imagery. He describes the false worship and the unclean rites which were carried on by the priests and leaders of the people in the subterranean chambers under the very foundations of the Temple. In the chambers above there was the form of worship of the true God, but in the chambers of imagery there was the worship of heathen gods. The angel said to Ezekiel in the parable vision: "Son of man, hast thou seen what the ancients of the house of Israel do in the dark, every man in the chambers of his imagery? for they say, The Lord seeth us not." (Ezek. 8:12.) Here one has a powerful sermon on the hidden life of the heart, without needing any outside illustrations.

As an illustration of lost opportunity, and particularly lost opportunity to break the power of temptation and sin in our lives, what could be more effective than the parable of the lost prisoner? Ahab had won a great victory over Benhadad, the king of Syria, and the inveterate enemy of Israel. But instead of destroying him or making certain that he could not renew the war in the near future, Ahab, puffed up with his victory, took Benhadad for a ride in his chariot and made a treaty of peace with him. Then came a "certain man of the sons of the prophets." Compelling a soldier to wound him in the head, and disguising his face with ashes, he sat moaning by the wayside as if he were a victim of the battle. As Ahab came driving by in his chariot, the wounded man hailed him. The king stopped and asked what he wanted. The man said, "Thy servant went out into the midst of the battle; and, behold, a man turned aside, and brought a man unto me, and said, Keep this man: if by any means he be missing, then shall thy life be for his life, or else thou shalt pay a talent of silver. And as thy servant was busy here and there, he was gone."

Hearing this tale, Ahab said to the supposed wounded soldier who had been faithless to his charge and let his prisoner escape, "So shall thy judgment be: thyself hast decided it." At that, the man of God took the ashes away from his face, and Ahab saw that he was one of the prophets. Then the prophet said to the king, "Thus saith the Lord, Because thou hast let go out of thy hand a man whom I appointed to utter destruction, therefore thy life shall go for his life, and thy people for his people." (I Kings 20:35-42.) What a powerful sermon on the subject of lost opportunity, and the danger of indulgence toward our temptations and besetting sins.

One of the most moving and dramatic of all the parables of the Bible is the story of the pet ewe lamb which the rich man took from the poor man and his children, and slaughtered for the entertainment of his guest. By this parable Nathan awoke the conscience of David and made him see his terrible transgression in the murder of Uriah and the adultery with Bathsheba. Perhaps that sentence of Nathan to David, when David's indignation was aroused at the monstrous cruelty of the rich man—that pointing of the finger, "Thou art the man"—is the most dramatic line in the Bible.

Whether familiar with them or not, people like to hear the stories of the Bible told and interpreted. And once told, the stories of the Bible leave their impression in the minds of those who hear them. Some of the great stories with which the preacher can always hold the people and tell them something worth while are: the story of Jacob, his deceit, his flight, his dreams, his romance with Rachel; Isaac and Abraham on Mount Moriah; Joseph and his brethren, perhaps the greatest of all stories; the stirring history of Gideon, and the incidents of David's life. And there is Jonah. What a story to preach on!

Sermons on the great characters of the Bible give opportunity for descriptive and pictorial preaching. When one tells these stories there is little need for outside illustration. The story itself is the best illustration. The preacher's task is to expand it and make it live so that it becomes a vivid reality to the congregation. A vigorous, imaginative presentation of any great Bible scene leaves a wholesome impression. I remember hearing a sermon on the Crucifixion. The preacher spent nearly the whole time describing the march of Jesus and the two thieves to Calvary, and then at the close he said just a few words on the Crucifixion. In the whole sermon there was hardly a single didactic statement of truth, and yet the sermon stirred me and others—and did us good. It was an example of how the mere description of a Bible scene is itself a powerful sermon.

One of the classic examples of biblical descriptive preaching is the description of the Crucifixion by James Waddel of Virginia, the father-in-law of Dr. Archibald Alexander, founder of Princeton Theological Seminary. The account of this sermon is found in William Wirt's well-known sketch of Waddel. He relates how he came to the wilderness church, where on a sacramental occasion the blind preacher was talking on the crucifixion of our Lord. Wirt thus describes the preacher and the sermon:

He then drew a picture of the sufferings of our Saviour; His trial before Pilate; His ascent up Calvary; His crucifixion, and His death. I know the whole history; but never, till then, had I heard the circumstances so selected, so arranged, so coloured. It was all new, and I seemed to have heard it for the first time in my life. His enumera-

tion was so deliberate that his voice trembled on every
syllable; every heart in the assembly trembled in unison.
His peculiar phrases had that force of description that the
original scene appeared to be, at that moment, acting before our eyes. We saw the very faces of the Jews; the
staring, frightful distortion of malice and rage. We saw
the buffet; my soul kindled with a flame of indignation,
and my hands were involuntarily and convulsively
clenched.

But when he came to touch on the patience, the forgiving meekness of our Saviour; when he drew, to the
life, His blessed eyes streaming in tears to heaven; His
voice breathing to God a soft and gentle prayer of pardon
on His enemies, "Father, forgive them, for they know not
what they do"—the voice of the preacher, which had all
along faltered, grew fainter and fainter; until now his utterance being obstructed by the force of his feelings, he
raised his handkerchief to his eyes and burst into a loud
and irrepressible flood of grief. The effect is inconceiva-
ble. The whole house resounded with the mingled groans
and sobs and shrieks of the congregation.

Another masterly example of biblical descriptive
preaching is a sermon on the healing of the demoniac
at Gadara preached by Christmas Evans, famous one-
eyed Welsh preacher. Historically the sermon is an
anachronism, since the preacher describes the home
town of the Gadarene as if it were some Welsh village.
But that, instead of marring the effect of the sermon,
actually makes it all the more vivid. The great medi-
eval painters, we may remember, presented scenes and

personalities of the Bible as if they were contemporary events and people of their own day in Italy, France, Germany, Spain, or Holland.

In the conclusion to this sermon on the demoniac at Gadara the preacher said:

Jesus commanded the legion of unclean spirits to come out of the man. They knew that out they must go. But they were like Scotchmen—very unwilling to return to their own country. They would rather go into hogs' skins than to their own country. And he suffered them to go into the herd of swine. Methinks that one of the men who fed the hogs kept a better lookout than the rest of them, and said, "What ails the hogs? Look sharp there, boys!— Keep them in!—Make good use of your whips. Why don't you run? Why, I declare, one of them has gone over the cliff! There goes another! Drive them back!" Never was there such a running, and whipping and hallooing; but down go the hogs, before they are aware of it. One of them said, "They are all gone!" "No, sure not all gone in the sea!" "Yes, every one of them, the black hog and all! They are all drowned—the devil is in them!"

And while they are talking, and everybody having something to say, homeward goes the man. As soon as he comes in sight of the house, I imagine I see one of his children running in and crying, "O mother! father is coming—he will kill us all!" "Children, come all into the house," says the mother, "Let us fasten the doors. I think there is no sorrow like my sorrow!" says the brokenhearted woman. "Are all the windows fastened, children?"

"Yes, mother." "Mary, my dear, come away from that window—don't be standing there." "Why, mother! I can hardly believe it is father! That man is well dressed." "O yes, my dear children, it is your own father. I knew him by his walk the moment I saw him." Another child stepping to the window says, "Why, mother, I never saw father coming home as he does today. He walks on the foot path and turns round the corner of the fence. He used to come towards the house as straight as a line, over fences, ditches, and hedges; I never saw him walking as slow as he does now."

Biography and Autobiography.—Whatever he reads, the preacher should include a great deal of biography, and especially autobiography. Such books are always out of the heart and true to life. Rousseau's *Confessions,* Augustine's *Confessions,* and *The Autobiography of Mark Rutherford* afford the preacher not only reading which will grip his soul but also striking and helpful illustrations for his sermon. For example, if one is preaching on conscience, there is a powerful illustration in Rousseau's *Confessions,* where he tells how he stole a ribbon while a guest at a nobleman's house in Italy and, when inquiry was made, charged one of the maids with the theft. To the end of his life, he said, he could remember the look of pain and reproach in the eyes of the beautiful and innocent girl whom he had accused.

In Augustine's *Confessions* there is a beautiful passage which shows how God can answer the sub-

41

stance of our prayer when he denies the particular thing for which we pray. The wayward Augustine planned to leave Africa and sail for Italy, to his mother's great distress and sorrow, since Monica feared that would be the end of him as far as his moral character was concerned. She earnestly entreated him with tears not to go, and pleaded with God to keep him from going. Augustine had his mother spend the night near the port at the hospice of St. Cyprian, telling her that he was going aboard the ship in the harbor just to say farewell to a friend. But when the morning came and Monica arose, both the ship and her wayward son were gone. The brokenhearted mother felt that her prayers had not been answered. The particular thing for which she had asked—that her son might be restrained from going to Italy—was not granted. But the object for which she prayed—the welfare and salvation of her son's soul—was achieved, since it was Augustine's visit to Italy which converted him to Christianity and brought about his mighty service to the Kingdom of Christ.

All kinds of biographies are stimulating and helpful to the preacher. I have never read any biography in which I did not come upon at least one incident or illustration which I could use in a sermon. Take a book like Andrew D. White's *Seven Great Statesmen*. In the chapter on Hugo Grotius there is a splendid passage which one can use when preaching on sin, repentance, or forgiveness. On his way back from a diplomatic errand in Sweden, the great humanitarian and Christian philosopher was shipwrecked off the Pomeranian coast. Badly battered by the sea, Grotius managed to get as far as the city of Rostock, where he lay down to die. When the young Lutheran pastor heard that Grotius was there he went to call on him. Feeling a natural embarrassment in talking to so great a man as Grotius about his soul, the young preacher just read to him our Lord's parable of the two men who went up to the temple to pray. He was reading how the publican, "standing afar off, would not lift up so much as his eyes unto heaven, but smote upon his breast, saying, God be merciful to me a sinner." At that, the dying Grotius lifted his hand and exclaimed, "That publican, Lord, am I."

There is a somewhat similar incident in the life of Copernicus, whose great book *The Revolution of the Heavenly Bodies* was placed in his hands just before he died. When he thought of his relationship to God, the famous astronomer saw himself only as an undeserving sinner, and directed that this epitaph—you can read it at Frauenburg—be placed on his grave: "O Lord, the faith thou didst give to St. Paul, I cannot ask; the mercy thou didst show to St. Peter, I dare not ask; but, Lord, the grace thou didst show unto the dying robber, that, Lord, show to me." When preaching on the penitent thief, nothing could be more effective than this incident from the death of the Polish astronomer.

In *Seven Great Statesmen* Dr. White relates how William M. Evarts was stricken with a serious eye disease. A specialist's verdict was total blindness within a short time. The noted orator and statesman received this news with composure: "Then I must go at once to Dresden and see the Sistine Madonna before it is too late." This is a timely and moving illustration on opportunity, or on the text, "The night cometh, when no man can work."

What about painters and paintings? Such illustrations must be used guardedly, for there has been a tendency to overdo them. However, there is no doubt that the study of some of the masterpieces dealing with biblical scenes and characters stirs the imagination of the preacher and helps him to make things real. There are often very effective stories about the painters and their works. This, in a sense, belongs to the field of biography. For example, the story of Leonardo da Vinci and the famous painting "The Last Supper." When the artist came to paint the face of Judas, he vented his hatred of a personal enemy by painting the man's features as the face of the betrayer. Those who came to watch him work immediately recognized Judas' face. But when he came to paint the face of Jesus, da Vinci seemed lost. Finally he realized that the spleen which he had vented on Judas' face prevented his painting the forgiving face of the Saviour. After he changed Judas' face he was able to paint Christ's face. Here is a striking illustration of how there can be no flowering of the Christian life and character when our hearts fester hatred toward a fellow man.

There is a moving story of Steinberg and the gypsy girl. Struck with her beauty, Steinberg took her to his studio and frequently had her sit for him. At that time he was at work on his masterpiece "Christ on the Cross." The girl used to watch him work on this painting. One day she said to him, "He must have been a very wicked man to be nailed to a cross like that." "No," said the painter. "On the contrary, he was a very good man. The best man that ever lived. He died for others." The little girl looked up at him and asked. "Did he die for you?" Steinberg was not a Christian, but the gypsy girl's question touched his heart and awakened his conscience, and he became a believer in him whose dying passion he had so well portrayed. Years afterward a young count chanced to go into the gallery at Dresden where Steinberg's painting of "Christ on the Cross" was on exhibition. This painting spoke so powerfully to him that it changed the whole tenor of his life. He was Count Nikolaus von Zinzendorf, founder of the Moravian Brethren.

There are some artists who are as much preachers as painters. To this class belongs George Frederic Watts with his wonderful symbolic picture of blindfolded Hope sitting on the globe, holding the broken lyre, just one string left. In the Tate Gallery, one can see his *Sic transit*. On the table in the center lies a shrouded form. Against the table leans a lyre. On a desk nearby is an open book. In one corner of the room is the ermine mantle of a peer, in the other the armor of a knight, with roses entwined about the spear to show that the sterner duties of life were mingled with the gentler things of art and sentiment. But all that is now past. The dead nobleman cannot don the mantle of his rank. He cannot draw the sword or hold the shield. He cannot read the book or awaken music from the lyre. All that is past. On the wall in the background are the three clauses of the old German proverb, "What I spent I had; what I saved I lost; what I gave I have." Nothing could be better than a description of that painting when the preacher is speaking on the true meaning of life. It can be used effectively in a commencement address.

Mythology—In his lectures *Revival and Preaching* Finney, the great evangelist of the nineteenth century, deprecates the use of ancient history and mythology in sermons. But there are many incidents and tales from old mythologies which bear well upon life and can be used to illustrate Christian truths. Gayley's *Classic Myths* is a book that every minister should have in his library. Suppose one is preaching on temptation. What is better than Homer's story of Ulysses and the palace of Circe and the white flower? With her magic wand the enchantress had turned all of Ulysses' companions into swine. Ulysses, armed with a white flower that one of the gods had given him, invaded Circe's palace. When she sought to change him also, he was able to resist her magic wand, and restore his companions to human form. Then there is another story of how Ulysses had his seamen bind him to the mast so that he could resist the songs of the sirens when the ship passed their island. In contrast, there is the story of the Argonauts, who, passing through dangerous waters where the beguiling and seductive sirens were wont to sing, had Orpheus play on his harp. Here is a splendid illustration of the truth that Christ in the heart is the best defense against temptation.

Preachers should know that great story of Theseus and Ariadne. When Theseus entered the Cretan Labyrinth to hunt out and slay the Minotaur, Ariadne put in his hand a silken thread. So long as he held that thread he could find his way out of the Labyrinth. So to the Christian, prayer is a golden thread. By holding it we pass safely through the dangerous temptations of life.

Fiction—It is a significant fact that in modern fiction—books spoken of as the "best sellers"—there is little that preachers can use to illustrate Christian truth. But the old masters will give the preacher much grist for his mill. Hawthorne is a great moralist, and almost all of his tales are forceful sermons. Most familiar, perhaps, is *The Scarlet Letter,* showing how sin always scars the heart. Then there is the powerful short story "The Minister's Black Veil." The congregation assembled in a New England church to greet their new minister. To their amazement, he appeared in the pulpit veiled in black. Some conjectured that his face was pocked with disease, the ravages of which he would hide from his people. Others said that he bore the burden of a recent bereavement. Still others thought that it was a token of penitence for sin.

Thus passed weeks, months, and years of a long pastorate. Never once was the black veil lifted. Finally when the minister lay dying on his bed, a neighboring minister who had come to pray with him begged him to lift the veil from his face that its secret might not go down with him into the grave.

The dying man raised himself in his bed and said, "Why do you tremble at me alone? Tremble also at each other! Have men avoided me, and women shown no pity, and children screamed and fled, only for my black veil? What, but the mystery which it obscurely typifies, has made this piece of crape so awful? When the friend shows his inmost heart to his friend; the lover to his best beloved; when man does not vainly shrink from the eye of his Creator, loathsomely treasuring up the secret of his sin; then deem me a monster, for the symbol beneath which I have lived, and die! I look around me, and, lo! on every visage A Black Veil!" The mystery which the black veil typified was secret and hidden sin.

When the preacher is talking of spiritual opportunity and the invitation of the Holy Spirit, what better can he do than to tell the story from Hawthorne's *The Marble Faun* of the specter and the catacombs: Memmius was a spy in the days of the last and the worst of the persecutions, that under Diocletian. His task was to spy out the Christians in their secret places of worship and bring them before the judges and the persecutors. Memmius was engaged in this infamous task, and was creeping stealthily along one of the narrow passages, when, suddenly, at a turning of the passage he came upon a little chamber where some Christians were met together. The candles were burning before the cross and the priest was standing before the altar. For a moment a divine indulgence was granted Memmius; if he had been capable of it, he might have bowed and received the everlasting light. But he hardened his heart, and those candles, symbols of the everlasting light, bewildered him with darkness, and the cross itself was stamped upon his heart as a sign that it should never open to conviction. Henceforth Memmius wandered through the catacombs seeking for some unwary visitor who would take him by the hand and lead him from darkness into light.

Charles Dickens' tales are well suited for use by the preacher, for he, too, was a great preacher. In *A Tale of Two Cities* there is nothing more moving than Dickens' description of Sydney Carton going up to his lonely lodgings and weeping on his unmade bed over his wasted life and lost opportunities. And yet at the end comes that beautiful scene of self-sacrifice when Carton, for the sake of the woman whom he has hopelessly loved, exchanges places with Darnay in the prison. As he rides in a cart to the guillotine, to give his life for another, there is a beautiful light in his face as in prophetic vision he sees the future happiness of the woman he loved in vain. Dickens' story of *Barnaby Rudge* is a wonderful study in conscience—

how the features of the murdered man, year after year, summer and winter, day and night, haunted the guilty man. If one is preaching on memory, good use can be made of Dickens' tale of the chemist who, troubled by his past, eagerly closed with an offer from the phantom who promised to relieve him of his remorse by taking away his memory. But as the days went by, the chemist found that what he thought would be a blessing had become a curse, and when the phantom reappeared he pleaded with him to dissolve his bargain and restore his memory. The story closes with the prayer, "Lord, keep my memory green!"

The tales of Victor Hugo abound in powerful illustrations for the preacher. In *Toilers of the Sea* there is a great passage on retribution.

The wicked Clubin had defrauded, cheated, and murdered, and yet had evaded justice. "He had kicked Rantaine into space, Lethierry into ruin, human justice into the darkness, opinion into error, all humanity away from himself. He had just eliminated the world." He had purposely wrecked his vessel on the rocks. He sent all the ship's company off in the long boat, to create the impression that he was going down with his ship like a hero, according to the tradition of the sea. Then with his ill-gotten 75,000 francs in a leather belt about him, he planned to swim to the Man Rock, hail a passing vessel, and leave behind him forever the scene of his crimes. He dived from the deck into the sea. Soon he felt himself dragged down under the water by a cold, clammy, steellike arm. It was the octopus!

Clubin had been punished. But his sin and punishment had not yet been uncovered before men. Months afterward, the heroic Gilliat sought to salvage the wreck. After he had slain the octopus which seized him in the cavern, he looked about him and saw a grinning skeleton encircled by a moldy leather belt. On the belt was the brass box, bright with the name Clubin on it, and with the stolen money in it. What had been covered in the abyss of hypocrisy and evil was brought to the surface. "There in the inexorable gloom of what might be called the encounter of hypocrisies, those two existences made up of waiting and of shadow, had come into violent collision; and one which was the beast had executed the other, which was the soul. Sinister justice!"

Poetry—So far as the quotation of poetry is concerned, there is almost none of it in the great preachers. They themselves in their imagination and fervor are their own poets. In quoting poetry the preacher runs the risk of sinking to the level of an entertainer or declaimer. The most effective use which can be made of the poets is to take some of their great scenes or incidents and present the truth which these illustrate. For example, if one is speaking on the futility of war or the meaning of life, he can use Robert Southey's poem "The Battle of Blenheim." The poet relates how, as old Caspar was sitting in the evening under a tree near the village of Blenheim, his little grandson brought a round smooth object which he had found near the brook. The old man explained that it was the skull of a soldier who had been killed in that great battle between the English and the French. The boy wanted to know more about the battle, so the old man took him on his knee and told him of its destruction and death and victory.

> "But what good came of it at last?"
> Quoth little Peterkin.
> "Why that I cannot tell," said he.
> "But 't was a famous victory."

There is an example of how the preacher can use an effective illustration from the poets. He need quote just a few lines, without any tax on his memory and without wearying his listeners.

Another good example of this method of illustration is Thomas Moore's story of "Paradise and the Peri" in *Lalla Rookh*. This can be used effectively in a sermon on prayer or repentance. The peri, banished from paradise, was refused admittance until she brought to the gate of heaven the most precious thing in God's sight. She went all over the world in quest of that treasure. First she brought the last drop of blood from the heart of a soldier dying on the battlefield for his country. But the custodian at the gate told her that would not avail. Then she brought a kiss of sacrificial love which a maid had implanted on the brow of her lover dying of the plague. But again the gate of heaven would not open. Then in the valley of Balbec she saw a little child kneeling in prayer by a fountain. As the child knelt, a man rode up on his horse and dismounted by the fountain to quench his thirst. His face was stamped with all manner of iniquity, crime, and sin. As he stooped to lift the water to his lips, his eye fell upon the little child kneeling in prayer. In a moment the hard face softened and changed, and a tear flowed down his cheek, for the man recalled the day when he, too, was innocent and prayed. It was that penitential tear that opened the gates of paradise to the banished peri.

A splendid illustration of retribution and how our sins come back to us is found in Southey's poem "The Inchcape Rock." In ancient times the abbot of the monastery at Aberbrothok had put a bell on this dangerous rock to warn incoming vessels. A roving pirate once sacked the town and cast the bell into the sea. Years afterward on a wild and stormy night this same pirate tried to steer his way into Aberbrothok harbor. But he listened in vain for the bell on the rock which would have given him his bearings, and he and his ship went down to an ocean grave. "As he had done, so God had requited him."

Philosophy—The reading of the philosophers will furnish the preacher with unusual, dignified, and searching illustrations. In Plato's *Republic* there is the famous description of the cave where men can see shadows of other men passing around them and above them. They can form only a very imperfect picture of the life these men lead. So in this life we have but an imperfect idea of the great realities of the heavenly life.

When preaching on the subject of immortality, judgment, and choice in life, one can use Plato's celebrated dream of Erus. Erus, the son of Armenius, was desperately wounded in battle in Pamphylia. When men came to bury the decomposing bodies, they found the body of Erus fresh and uncorrupted. They carried it to his home and prepared it for burial. On the twelfth day Erus revived as he lay on his funeral pyre, and related what he had seen in the other world. After his soul had left the body he went with a great company to a mysterious place on the borders of heaven and earth. In the earth there were two great gaps, and opposite them similar gaps in heaven. A never-ceasing stream of souls passed up out of the earth toward heaven and down from heaven to the earth. At the two gaps the judges sat on their thrones, and there the stream of souls coming from the earth was divided into two great companies, the just being commanded to take the road to the right leading up to heaven, and the unjust the road to the left—leading downward to the earth. The just bore placards declaring their virtues, the unjust placards telling of their sins. When Erus' turn came to appear before the judges, they told him that he should be a witness of all that took place after the judgment, and return to earth to tell his fellow men all that he had seen.

Perhaps we can think of Addison also as a philosopher. When the preacher speaks on the subject of burdens, he can do nothing better than make use of Addison's tale of the angel and the burdens. Writing on the remark of Socrates—how if all the misfortunes of mankind were cast into a public stock and equally distributed among men, those who now think themselves the most unhappy would prefer the share they already have to that which would fall to them by such a division—Addison relates a dream he once had. In this he heard a proclamation by Jupiter that every mortal should bring in his griefs and calamities and throw them together in a heap. Into the central plain marched the whole army of mankind, led on by an airy figure named Fancy, and laid down their burden of real or imagined woe. Slowly the heap of discarded burdens grew until it reached to the heavens.

Then Jove issued a second proclamation that everyone was now at liberty to take up any burden he might choose. Fancy stood near and recommended to each one his particular packet. The deluded mortals eagerly rushed into the most foolish and absurd bargains. But when each one had selected his new burden, the whole plain was filled with lamentations and murmurings, for everyone thought that his last state was worse than his first.

Taking pity on them, Jove ordered them to lay down their burdens a second time, so that each might reassume his own. Fancy was commanded to disappear, and a new figure, the goddess Patience, stood by the mountain of misery, which immediately sank to such a degree that it did not seem a third the size it was before. Each man then took up his burden, well pleased that the kind of burden which was to fall to his lot had not been left to his own choice. Men have their own burdens, and their own burdens are best suited to them.

The Danish philosopher Kierkegaard is often very difficult to read. He reminds one somewhat of the old definition of philosophical preaching—one man telling what he does not know to another man who does not understand what he is talking about. But in Kierkegaard's parable of the wild duck there is a splendid illustration of how the soul declines from its ideals and becomes satisfied with lower standards. With his mates this duck was flying in the springtime northward across Europe. During the flight he came down in a Danish barnyard where there were tame ducks. He enjoyed some of their corn. He stayed, for an hour, then for a day, then for a week, then for a month, and finally, because he relished the good fare and the safety of the barnyard, he stayed all summer. But one autumn day when the flock of wild ducks were winging their way southward again, they passed over the barnyard, and their mate heard their cries. He was stirred with a strange thrill of joy and delight, and with a great flapping of wings he rose in the air to join his old comrades in their flight.

But he found that his good fare had made him so soft and heavy that he could rise no higher than the eaves of the barn. So he dropped back again to the barnyard, and said to himself, "Oh well, my life is safe here and the food is good." Every spring and autumn when he heard the wild ducks honking, his eyes would gleam for a moment and he would begin to flop his wings. But finally the day came when the wild ducks flew over him and uttered their cry, but he paid not the slightest attention to them. What a parable that is of how the soul can forget its high ideals and standards and be content with lower things!

Nature and Common Life—Here the great Exemplar is our Lord himself. He was always saying, "The kingdom of heaven is like unto"—the seed sown in the ground, the wheat and the tares, the plowman who came upon the hidden treasure, the mustard tree, the woman who put the leaven in the lump, the woman who searched for the lost coin, the merchant who bought the goodly pearl, the lilies of the field, the birds of the air, and the hen covering her chickens with her wing. For myself, I have always felt that while Christ in his divine simplicity could effectively use such illustrations, the ordinary preacher runs a certain risk in their use. Neither have I ever felt that the ordinary scientific illustration about the processes of growth or about the universe is effective. There is a kind of laboratory schoolroom flavor about them. When we speak of Christ and his illustrations from nature, we must remember that this was not the only source of his illustrations. He also made his teachings luminous by illustrations from history, such as the brazen serpent and the power of the cross to save by faith, Jonah's deliverance and his own resurrection. He made use of current events in Palestinian life, such as the fall of the tower of Siloam, and Pilate's mingling the blood of the Galileans with the blood of their sacrifices.

One of William Jennings Bryan's most effective passages was a paragraph on immortality in his lecture "The Prince of Peace," in which he draws his metaphors from nature.

If the Father deigns to touch with divine power, the cold and pulseless heart of the buried acorn and makes it burst forth from its prison walls, will he leave neglected in the earth the soul of man made in the image of his Creator? If He stoops to give to the rose bush whose withered blossoms float upon the autumn breeze the sweet assurance of another spring, will He refuse the words of hope to the sons of men when the frost of winter comes? If matter, mute and inanimate, though changed by the forces of nature into a multitude of forms can never die, will the imperial spirit of man suffer annihilation when it has paid a brief visit like a royal guest to this tenement of clay?

Beecher was very fond of illustrations from nature and knew far more about seeds, grasses, flowers, and plants than the average man. Some of his most effective illustrations are in his sermon "The Ages to Come." He illustrates our inability in our present state of knowledge to forecast the glories of heaven by comparing us to a man who comes into the world with a ripe experience, but who has never seen an October, and showing how impossible it would be for him to foretell the colors of autumn from the first budding growth of spring. An Eskimo who had seen only sand, moss, stunted shrubs, winter berries, and glacier flowers, could form no idea of the magnificent parasitic plants which fill the tropical forests. Shivering in midsummer under icebergs, he could have no conception of the everlasting pomp and glory of the equatorial regions. So the reality of the heavenly life unspeakably transcends any conception which mortal man may form of it.

Metaphors—Some of the greatest preachers have been metaphorical preachers. They made no use of anecdotes or formal illustrations, but their very language was pictorial and descriptive. They understood, or had an unconscious instinct for, the witchery of words.

> Words are the silver notes
>   That ring the chord of sound,
> And play the colored symphony of speech.

Beecher was definitely a metaphorical preacher. So was Talmage. One of the most famous speeches in American oratory was William Jennings Bryan's at the 1896 Democratic convention, when he brought delegates cheering to their feet with his celebrated metaphor borrowed from the Crucifixion, "You shall not press down upon the brow of labor this crown of thorn. You shall not crucify mankind upon a cross of gold." A splendid example of effective illustration in the form of a metaphor or simile is found in Charles Kingsley's sermon "Temptation," drawn from the story of Ahab and Naboth's vineyard, "There is a state of mind which is a bird call for all the devils, and when they see a man in this state of mind, they flock around him like crows around carrion." Here is one of Talmage's quick flashes by way of comparison. Preaching on the futility of expostulating with the slanderer, he says, "You might as well read the Ten Commandments to a flock of crows."

Personal Experience—The preacher always runs some risk when he uses his own personal experiences for illustrations. If the personality of the preacher is presented too often to his congregation it is apt to lose stature. When Michelangelo was painting his Jonah and the other prophets and sibyls on the ceiling of the Sistine Chapel, he had a candle stuck in a pasteboard cap on his forehead. It threw light on his work, but kept his own shadow from obstructing it. That is the way the preacher should use his own experiences. The purpose is to throw light on the truth and on other characters, but not on himself.

There is no doubt that wisely-selected illustrations from personal experience will often be very effective. If a man has had a godly home and godly parents, references to that home and to his parents will always be acceptable and timely. Talmage did a great deal of that. In his sermon "The Fast Young Man" he speaks of the garments that mothers make for their sons, and says, "You remember just how the hands looked, the roughness of the ends of the fingers from the touch of the needle; the color of the veins on the back of the hands. Alas, that hand is stilled forever!" In another sermon, "The King's Wagons" (Gen. 45:27), he gives a beautiful description of his father and mother coming home from church on a stormy Sabbath day. At twelve o'clock they would go to the window to see if their father and mother were coming, and then at half past twelve and then at one o'clock. "After a while Mary or Daniel or DeWitt would shout: 'The wagon's coming!' And then we would see it wind out of the woods and over the brook and through the lane and up in front of the old farm house, and then we would rush out, leaving the doors wide open, and, with many things to tell them, asking them questions."

Sometimes when preaching on heaven and the happy reunion there, I have related an experience of my childhood. At the end of a summer day, returning from some expedition into the country, my brothers and I, driving in the carriage or the spring wagon, would cross a stone bridge over a brook, and then go up a hill through the woods. On the shoulder of the hill, as we turned to go down toward the river, we could see our large frame house standing on the bluff, and almost always we could see a napkin, handkerchief, or towel fluttering from the eastern window of my father's study on the second story. It was our mother waiting for the return of her children and waving us that far-off welcome. So we like to think

that our loved ones who have gone before us to prepare a place will be there at heaven's window waving
us a welcome.

ILLUSTRATIONS AS INTRODUCTIONS OR CONCLUSIONS

Charles Wolfe, author of those almost perfect
lines, "The Burial of Sir John Moore"—

> We buried him darkly at dead of night,
> The sods with our bayonets turning,
>
> .   .   .   .
>
> We carved not a line, and we raised not a stone,
> But we left him alone with his glory—

was also a preacher of originality and power. On the
subject of the introduction to a sermon he said, "Bring
in familiar topics. Begin naturally and easily, but so
as to excite curiosity, with an incident or an anecdote.
Begin in an original or striking, but sedate manner."
If one preaches on some Bible character or incident,
the Bible narrative makes an easy, natural, and successful introduction to the sermon.

Thomas Guthrie is a master in the use of illustrations at the beginning of a sermon. In his sermon "The
Sins and Sorrows of the City" he describes how a
man might see in the ocean under his boat on a quiet
day "the standing stumps of trees and the moulder-
ing vestiges of a forest where once the wild cat
prowled and the birds of heaven, singing their loves,
had nestled and nursed their young. . . . The same phe-
nomenon could be seen in our great cities. Not a sin-

gle house or a block of houses, but whole streets had been engulfed. A flood of ignorance and sin now breaks and roars above the tops of their highest tenements."

A good example of anecdote or illustration at the beginning of a sermon is found in Canon Liddon's sermon "The First Five Minutes After Death." He tells of a retired army officer who had returned from India, to spend his last days in England. One day his friends persuaded him to give an account of his life and service in India. They listened with breathless interest to the account of his battles and sieges and his experiences in the Sepoy Mutiny. At the conclusion he said, "I expect to see something more thrilling than anything I have seen yet." His hearers were surprised at that, since they knew that he was well past seventy and had retired from active service. After a pause he added in an undertone, "I mean the first five minutes after death!"

Suppose one is preaching a sermon on Absalom's pillar, the beautiful tomb that was never used because his dishonored body lay beneath the stones which David's soldiers had cast upon it in the wood of Ephraim. A striking and arresting illustration to begin this sermon would be a description of the monument on the Saratoga battlefield, with the figures of Generals Gates, Schuyler, and Morgan, who took part in that great battle, set in the niches at the base. "But the fourth niche stands empty," the preacher might say. "The soldier who won that niche of fame has forfeited his right to be remembered. Below the empty niche there is a solitary name cut in the stone, and as the eye falls upon it a vision rises. I see a young Colonial officer leading his troops on a wintry morning against the battlements of Quebec. Again I see him charging the British lines at Saratoga, and yet again crouching at the midnight hour by the murmuring Hudson, bartering his soul to Satan. The scene changes. I see a lonely room in London and an old man dying. He is friendless, homeless, and forsaken—Benedict Arnold, hero, patriot, and traitor."

When preaching on Absalom and his vacant monument, or on the text "Thou shalt be missed," the same kind of introduction can be used by describing the shields of noted American soldiers in the cadet chapel at West Point. The shield of Benedict Arnold bears just the dates of his birth and death, but no name. The same illustration could be used also when one preaches on the missing tribe in heaven. The tribes of Israel are spoken of in the book of Revelation as having been sealed by the angel of God. Only the tribe of Dan is missing. The illustration also fits Judas Iscariot. The wall of the city has twelve foundations and in them the names of the twelve apostles. But the name of Judas is missing.

Too often the conclusion of the sermon is neglected. The preacher spends all his enthusiasm and energy in the introduction and body of the sermon and has nothing left for the conclusion. Many a sermon has no real end. Sometimes a well-chosen illustration will make an effective conclusion. The masterpiece in this respect is the Sermon on the Mount, which comes to a conclusion with our Lord's illustration of the two houses, the house which was built on a rock and stood firm when the floods came and the rain descended and the winds blew and beat upon it, and the house which was built upon the sand and fell when the storm came, and great was the fall of it.

Frederick W. Robertson has a strong and appealing conclusion in his sermon on the text, "Considering thyself, lest thou also be tempted." Here he uses a series of interrogations, sometimes the best way in which to close a sermon. But along with his interrogations is a striking illustrative metaphor:

Or art thou in all these points simply untried? Proud Pharisee of a woman who passes by an erring sister with a haughty look of conscious superiority, doest thou know what temptation is? With strong feeling and mastering opportunity shall the rich-cut crystal which stands on the table of the wealthy man, protected from dust and injury, boast that it has escaped the flaws and the cracks and the fractures which the earthen jar has sustained, exposed and subjected to rough and general uses? O man or woman, thou who wouldst be a Pharisee, consider, O consider thyself, lest thou also be tempted.

When one discusses providence and predestination, or the problem of evil and pain in the world, a good way to conclude would be to relate a legend from the *Gesta Romanorum:*

A hermit and an angel once set out on a journey together. The angel was in human form and garb, but had told the hermit about his exalted rank. The first night they stopped at a humble home by the wayside, where, for the love of God, they were granted food and shelter. In the middle of the night the angel strangled the infant child of their host. The hermit was horrified at this deed, but since he knew his companion was an angel he kept silent. At the end of the next day's journey they were entertained at a city mansion, and when they departed the angel stole the beautiful golden cup from which his host had drunk the wine at dinner.

On the next day's journey they were crossing a bridge over a deep and dangerous stream when they met a pilgrim. The angel said to the pilgrim, "Canst thou show us, good father, the way to the next town?" When the pilgrim turned to point out the road, the angel picked him up and flung him over the parapet into the river. Seeing that, the hermit said to himself, "Surely this is a devil with whom I travel, for all his works are evil!" But he said nothing to the angel.

As the darkness came on that night, the snow was falling, and they heard the howling of wolves in the forest. In the distance they saw a light in a cottage window and, knocking at the door, they asked for refuge. The surly master of the house cursed them away. "Yonder is the pigsty. That is the place for dirty beggars like you!" So they passed the night in the pigsty among the swine. In the morning the angel went to the man's house and thanked him for his hospitality. For a keepsake he gave him the golden goblet.

Then the hermit could no longer restrain his anger. "Get thee gone, wretched spirit!" he cried. "Thou pretendest to be a messenger from heaven, yet thou requitest good with evil, and evil with good."

The angel looked upon him with compassionate eyes: "Hark, thou short-sighted mortal. For love of that infant son the father had been made covetous, breaking God's commandments by heaping up wealth for his boy, which the boy, if he had lived, would have wasted in riotous living and debauchery. My act, which seemed to you so cruel, saved both parent and child. The owner of the golden goblet which I took had once been abstemious, but he was becoming a drunken sot. The loss of his cup has set him to thinking, and he will mend his ways. The poor pilgrim whom I threw into the river was about to commit a mortal sin when I interfered and sent his soul unsullied to heaven. As for this wretch who drove God's children from his door, he is, indeed, pleased for the moment with the bauble I have given him, but hereafter he will burn in hell."

When the hermit heard these words he bowed his head and murmured, "Forgive me, Lord, that in my ignorance I misjudged thee."

Although the ways of providence are often inscrutable to us, one day we shall be able to see what we can now behold only by faith, that

There's a wideness in God's mercy,
Like the wideness of the sea;

.   .   .   .

And the heart of the Eternal
Is most wonderfully kind.

ILLUSTRATIONS FROM IMAGINATION

The average preacher does not make enough use of his imagination. He can use it either in describing a Bible scene or in a flight of pure fancy. He can repeat an imaginary conversation between two Bible characters, or visualize a scene or episode in heaven. A good example of a preacher's imagination used to embellish and make vivid a scriptural narrative is found in the introduction to Talmage's sermon on "The King's Wagons." The sermon commences with a description of the capital of the Pharaohs:

There were temples aflame with red sandstone, entered by gateways that were guarded by pillars, bewildering with hieroglyphics, and wound with brazen serpents, and adorned with winged creatures, their eyes and beaks and pinions glittering with precious stones. There were marble columns blooming into white flower buds. There were stone pillars, the tops bursting into the shapes of lotus when in full bloom. Along the avenues lined with sphinx and fane and obelisk, there were princes who came in gorgeously upholstered palanquins, carried by servants in scarlet, or else were drawn in vehicles with snow white horses, golden-bitted, six abreast, dashing at full run.

68

There were fountains from stone-wreathed vases, climbing the ladder of the sun.

An instance of Whitefield's power of description and imagination is the story how he was preaching one day at his tabernacle, and Chesterfield, sitting in Lady Huntingdon's pew, heard him liken a sinner to a blind beggar passing along a dangerous road near a cliff. The beggar's little dog ran away, and he was left alone to probe the perilous path with his iron-shod staff. Finally he groped to the edge of the precipice and dropped his staff into the abyss. Unaware of his danger, the blind man stooped down to retrieve his staff and hurtled forward over the edge. So strong was Whitefield's description that Chesterfield leaped to his feet, crying out, "Great God! he's gone!"

At the conclusion of his sermon on "Enoch," Bishop Simpson lets himself go in a flight of noble imagination. He first describes Infidelity conducting the Soul through the earth, showing him the beauties and splendors of the world, the rocks and fossils and the stories they tell of ancient catastrophes. Then Infidelity conducts the Soul into the heavens and shows him the solar system and goes with him from planet to planet until they reach the last star in the suburbs of the universe. There the Soul sits down and, looking up into the face of his guide, asks, "Is this all?" Surprised at this, Infidelity asks, "Is it not enough?" The Soul says something is yet lacking.

Infidelity then leaves him, and Christianity comes to

his side. She leads him through the same wonders in heaven above, on the earth beneath, and in the waters under the earth. When they have reached the last star, he gazes into the face of his guide and asks again, "Is this all?" With a look of pity, and yet of love, his guide exclaims, "Is this all! This is but the portico. It is the entrance to the Father's House." Christianity puts the glass of faith in the Soul's hand, and he cries: "I look through it, and away beyond the stars, away beyond the multiplied systems, I see the great Center, the Throne of God, about which all things move, the great Central point of the Universe; and as I look, there is One upon the Throne. He is my Brother; and I look again, and my name is written on His hands, and I cry out with ecstasy:

> 'Before the throne my Surety stands,
> My name is written on His hands.' "

Imagination can be expressed in the form of an apostrophe. When Eliphalet Nott preached the famous sermon on dueling which did so much to arouse Christian sentiment against the practice, after the fatal duel between Alexander Hamilton and Aaron Burr, he commenced with this apostrophe to the angels:

Withdraw, therefore, for a moment, ye celestial spirits —ye spirits—ye holy angels accustomed to hover round these altars, and listen to those strains of grace which heretofore have filled this house of God. Other subjects occupy us. Withdraw, therefore, and leave us; leave us to exhort Christian parents to restrain their vengeance, and at least to keep back their hands from blood.

David Hume said it was worth going twenty miles to hear Whitefield and see one of those geyser-like jets of spontaneous passion and emotion. Hume declared:

Once after a solemn pause he thus addressed his audience: "The attendant angel is just about to leave the threshhold of the Sanctuary and to ascend to Heaven. And shall he ascend and not bear with him the news of one sinner among all this multitude reclaimed from the error of his ways? Stop, Gabriel; stop, ere you enter the sacred portals, and yet carry with you the news of one sinner converted to God!"

Samuel Davies, Presbyterian minister at Hanover, Virginia, and afterward president of Princeton, was a great Colonial preacher. In one of his flights of imagination he pictures a lost soul meeting its body in the resurrection. Both soul and body heap bitter recriminations upon each other. The soul says to the body:

And must I be chained to thee again, O thou accursed, polluted body, thou system of deformity and terror! In thee I once sinned, by thee I was once ensnared, debased, and ruined; to gratify thy vile lusts and appetites I neglected my own immortal interests, degraded my native dignity, and made myself miserable forever. And hast thou now met me to torment me forever? O that thou hadst still slept in the dust, and never been repaired again!

71

Then the body answers:

Come, guilty soul, enter thy old mansion; if it be horrible and shocking, it is owing to thyself. . . . My knees would have bowed at the throne of grace, but thou didst not affect the posture. Mine eyes would have read, and mine ears heard the Word of Life, but thou wouldst not set them to that employ. And now it is but just the body thou didst prostitute to sin should be the instrument of thy punishment. . . . Therefore, come, miserable soul, take possession of this frame, and let us prepare for everlasting burning. Oh, that it were now possible to die! Oh, that we could be again separated, and never be united more! Vain wish; the weight of mountains, the pangs of hell, the flames of unquenchable fire, can never dissolve these chains which now bind us together!

For a daring journey into the realm of imagination Chalmers gives us a good example in his famous sermon "The Expulsive Power of a New Affection." His purpose is to sum up the thought of the sermon—that the mere demonstration of the world's vanity is not sufficient to win the heart from the love of the world, and that there must be set forth another object more worthy of its attachment. He pictures a man standing on the verge of this pleasant world, surveying all its glories and beauties, and then looking off into the abyss of space:

Think you that he would bid a voluntary adieu to all this brightness and all the beauty that were before him upon earth, and commit himself to the frightful solitude away from it? Would he leave its peopled dwelling places, and become a solitary wanderer through the fields of nonentity? But if, during the time of his contemplation, some happy island of the blest had floated by; and there had burst upon his senses the light of its surprising glories, and its sounds of sweeter melody; and could he further see that pain and mortality were there unknown; and above all, that signals of welcome were hung out and an avenue of communication was made for him—perceive you not, that what was before the wilderness, would become the land of invitation; and that now the world would be the wilderness?

One of Talmage's most frequently preached sermons was "All Heaven Looking On," from the text, "Seeing we also are compassed about with so great a cloud of witnesses." (Heb. 12:1.) He likens our battle in life to a Roman amphitheater where thousands watched the gladiators and martyrs fight the beasts. The Christian, too, must fight with beasts—the lions and tigers of appetite and sin. But he does not fight alone. A cloud of witnesses looks down upon him. Talmage first describes the gallery of angels, naming nearly all the great angels of the Bible, from the angel that swung his sword at the gate of Eden to the angel of the Incarnation, and finally all the seraphim and cherubim of heaven. All these angels are man's friends in his struggle with the beast.

Then he describes the gallery of prophets and apostles—Hosea, David, Jeremiah, Daniel, Isaiah, Peter, Paul, Moses, and Noah—all cheering the Christian on.

73

Daniel cries out, "Thy God will deliver thee from the mouth of the lion." David says, "He will not suffer thy foot to be moved." Isaiah counsels, "Fear not, I am with thee." Paul promises, "Victory through our Lord Jesus Christ." Then comes the gallery of martyrs —Latimer, the Theban Legion, and Felicitas, who encouraged her children while they died for the faith. Then comes the gallery of great Christians—Martin Luther, Lyman Beecher, John Calvin, George Whitefield, Charles Wesley, David Brainerd, Adoniram Judson, and finally Isaac Watts, who exhorts the Christian struggling in the arena to sing:

> Must I be carried to the skies
> On flowery beds of ease,
> While others fought to win the prize
> And sailed through bloody seas?

Then comes the gallery of our departed kin— father, mother, children—all encouraging us to be faithful unto death.

Years ago I chanced to talk with a classmate of Talmage at the New Brunswick Theological Seminary. I asked him what the great preacher was like in his seminary days. He said he spoke and preached exactly as he did in the days of his fame. He recalled his class sermon on the text, "There is a friend that sticketh closer than a brother." (Prov. 18:24.) Talmage described the scene in heaven when Christ set out on his mission of redemption. The astonished angels said to him: "Shall ten thousand of us weave our wings to-

74

gether to make a fit chariot for thee to ride upon in thy descent to that fallen world?" This offer Christ rejected with a wave of his hand. The angels then exclaimed, "Shall we bring together all the clouds of heaven and make a fit throne for thee to sit upon?" But this offer Christ also refused: "No, I cannot go in such a way." Then they asked if they might not make a platform out of their wings and so conduct him to earth? For the third time Christ refused. Then he commanded them, "Take off these royal robes." The angels reluctantly obeyed. Then he started alone on his descent to earth, without any of his royal insignia, without a single attendant. The amazed angel host crowded on heaven's vast balcony to see him descend, and as they gazed after him, they talked so loudly together about his wonderful condescension and love for men that the shepherds of Bethlehem heard them!

The mind of man delights in a stirring scene or spectacle, whether it is a battlefield of temptation or an imaginary scene of triumph and glory in the heavenly places. Let the preacher remember this, and throw open as wide as he can the golden gates of imagination. Napoleon said, "Men of imagination rule the world." The preacher of imagination is the prince of the pulpit.

III

GETTING READY FOR THE PULPIT

Once in the dim, gas-lighted recesses of the old mercantile Library on Ninth Street, Philadelphia, I came across the Rev. Dr. John R. Davies, the eloquent and successful minister of the Bethlehem Presbyterian Church on Broad Street. We talked together about reading and preparation for the pulpit. I remember what he said to me about his own method. It was this: "I find the best plan is to read widely during the week in many fields and in many books, and then toward the end of the week, when I begin to prepare definitely for the sermons on Sunday, it is just like opening the faucet at a fountain or sink, and the water for the sermon flows easily out."

Perhaps some would regard that as a dangerous method, unless they possess the particular gifts which marked the man who prescribed it. But this much certainly is true—wide reading in any worth-while field stimulates the mind and gives the reader something of use to him when he comes to prepare his sermon. As Bacon put it, "Reading maketh a full man."

BIBLE READING

But what to read? That is the question. First of all, there must be regular devotional reading of the Bible.

76

The minister's morning and evening portion are, as in the case of every other reader of the Bible, for his own personal spiritual nourishment and growth in grace, and we dare not neglect that in our preparation for the pulpit. But in that regular and devotional reading, the minister will also equip himself in a special way for the preparation and preaching of his sermons. First of all, he will gain an ever-increasing familiarity with the text of the Holy Scriptures, with which no one, and especially no minister, can be too familiar. Even in the case of one who has long been a reader of the Bible and expounder of the word, there will be books or sections of books in the Bible with which he has little familiarity.

The minister ought to be familiar with all the books of the Bible and all parts of every book. It is easy to pass over books like Ezra, Leviticus, Chronicles, Lamentations, and some of the minor prophets. If preachers took an examination on the book of Revelation, many would be surprised to find that the only portion with which they are really familiar is at the end where the beauty of the holy city, the new Jerusalem, is described—the excerpt which is read at the funeral service—and perhaps portions from the letters to the Seven Churches. If, for example, the preacher were to skip I Chronicles, he would never discover that gem of a miniature biography upon which we come in the midst of a dreary genealogical table, the notice of Jabez—"more honorable than his brethren"

—who "called on the God of Israel, saying, Oh that thou wouldest bless me indeed, and enlarge my coast, and that thine hand might be with me, and that thou wouldest keep me from evil, that it may not grieve me!" There is a fragrant and delicate flower, still blooming after all these ages in that dust heap of long-forgotten names. Neither would the minister who left out Chronicles come upon that fine text for a sermon at the end or the beginning of the year, the last verse of the last chapter, and the last historical word in the Bible about David, "All his reign and his might, and the times that went over him, and over Israel, and over all the kingdoms of the countries."

These are examples of the worth-whileness of thorough and complete Bible reading. Of course, if a preacher merely follows the trail of other preachers, and takes a text because someone else has used it, then he might get along without such reading. But that would be a low order of preaching.

As one reads the Bible, even at devotional periods, it is helpful to mark verses or incidents which make a particular appeal to him at that time. It is my custom to put a check in the margin opposite any such verse. When I happen on these marked passages again, some of them may not appeal to me as suitable texts or suggestions for a sermon, as they did at first, but others will still appeal. In this methodical reading we are apt to come upon bits of history or fragments from a biography which strike us as suitable for a sermon.

That is the way texts and sermon thoughts from the Bible accumulate.

GENERAL READING

What shall a man read? First of all, he ought to read a good newspaper. This will keep him informed of current events. The daily reading of a newspaper is greatly to be preferred to relying on any of the popular digests of the news of the day. The preacher ought to be his own "digester," and select for himself the world's events and movements that are worth noting. Newspapers are always in touch with human life. In their columns the minister sees the tragedy, the glory, the wretchedness, the suffering, and the pathos of mankind. When an item seems to have possible sermon value, the minister should put it aside in a place where he can find it when he wants it. But I shall come to that later.

Probably the most helpful reading for the minister —that is, general reading—is history and biography, especially biography. There you have life, not in theory, but in reality. You can hear the beating of the human heart when you read biography. To a less degree, this is true of history. Planned reading is good. I remember Dr. Francis L. Patton telling us how in his first pastorate he carefully read through Gibbon's *History of the Decline and Fall of the Roman Empire*. Some reading in philosophy is also valuable if the preacher can keep himself from the temptation to think that he is a philosopher, and not fall into the sad error of preaching *about* truth and *about* life instead of preaching to living men. Fiction, if carefully chosen to avoid the trivial and filthy, of which there is so much in our day, can stimulate the minister's mind. Dickens, Hawthorne, and Victor Hugo represent the type of fiction helpful to the preacher, both to stir his mind and to illustrate the truths of the gospel. Poetry also is good, for it stimulates the imagination, a faculty sadly neglected by the majority of preachers. Probably we all read more poetry in our early years than in our later ones, but the preacher ought never to part company with the poets. The objective is not to quote poetry in sermons—there is altogether too much of this—but to find worth-while sermon ideas, situations, and illustrations from the great poets.

Naturally, the minister will have some formal works of theology at hand. I remember Dr. Patton telling us that he never preached a sermon on one of the great doctrines of the Christian faith without getting down Hodge's *Systematic Theology* to see what that great theologian had to say on the subject. This was in striking contrast to the attitude of a minister I encountered not long after leaving the seminary who actually boasted that he had traded his Hodge for a box of cigars.

In answer to requests as to what books the minister ought to have in his library, I once mailed to a number of inquirers the following list of books which I myself have found helpful—the only ground on which one can recommend books to another:

80

Poetry: Cambridge editions of the English poets, *Saint Paul,* by F. W. H. Myers, *American Anthology,* by Stedman, *Oxford Book of Victorian Verse,* poems of Stephen Phillips, Matthew Arnold, A. E. Housman, translations of the *Iliad* and *Odyssey.*

Sermons by Beecher, Spurgeon, F. W. Robertson, Finney, Liddon, Ambrose Shepherd, G. G. Selby, Watkinson, James Walker, C. J. Vaughn, Father Stanton, Talmage, Chrysostom, Christmas Evans, Dean Swift, Robert Hall, Dean Farrar, Guthrie, Irving; also *World's Great Sermons* (ten volumes), and *Great Sermons of the World* (compiled by Macartney).

Homiletics: The Throne of Eloquence by Paxton Hood, *Psychic Power in Preaching* by Kennard, *History of Oratory* by Sears, *Princes of the Christian Pulpit* by Howard, *Homiletics* by J. M. Hoppin, *Homiletics* by Vinet, *Sons of Thunder* and *Kings of the American Pulpit* by Macartney.

Apologetics: Natural Theology by Paley, *Foundations of Belief* by Balfour, *Fundamental Christianity* by Patton, *History of Rationalism* by Hurst, *Moral Truths of Christianity* by Luthardt.

Theology: Creeds of Christendom by Schaff, *Theism* by Flint, *Lectures* by A. A. Hodge, *Philosophy of the Future State* by Dick, *Virgin Birth* by Machen, *Evolution* by Moore, *The Atonement* by Campbell, *The Atonement* by Dale, *The Atonement* by Stocker, *The Lamb of God* by Nicol, *Systematic Theology* by Finney, and the works of Jonathan Edwards.

Devotional: Saints' Everlasting Rest by Baxter, *Pilgrim's Progress* by Bunyan, Augustine's *Confessions, Let-*

ters to Men by Fenelon, *Rise and Progress of Religion* by Doddridge, *Imitation of Christ* by Thomas à Kempis, *Holy Living* and *Holy Dying* by Taylor.

Hymnology: Story of the American Hymn by Ninde, *Studies of Familiar Hymns* by Benson, *Latin Hymns* by March (in Latin).

History: Church history by Neander, Schaff; *Ten Epochs of Church History;* histories of the United States by Rhodes, Bancroft, and McMaster; *Lincoln* by Nicolay and Hay (ten volumes), *History of the English People* by Greene, *History of England* by Hume, *Historian's History of the World, Rome* by Momsen, *Decline and Fall of the Roman Empire* by Gibbon, *Conquest of Mexico* by Prescott, *Rise of the Dutch Republic* by Motley, *Conquest of Granada* and *Conquest of Spain* by Washington Irving.

Religious biography: Lives of Christ by Farrar, David Smith, Geike, Beecher; *Lives of Paul* by David Smith, Farrar, Ramsey, F. J. Foakes-Jackson, Conybeare; *Origin of Paul's Religion* by Machen, *Greater Men and Women of the Bible* by Hastings, *Bible Characters* by Whyte.

Commentaries: Ellicott, Henry, Lange, *Sermon Bible, The Four Gospels* by David Smith, *Holy Scriptures* by Gore, *Topical Bible* by Nave, *People's Bible, Speaker's Commentary.*

Dictionaries and encyclopedias: Davis' *Bible Dictionary;* Hastings' *Dictionary of the Bible, Dictionary of Christ and the Gospels,* and *Encyclopaedia of Religion and Ethics, Encyclopaedia Britannica, Encyclopedia Americana, Dictionary of American Biography.*

For quick reference: Bartlett's Quotations, Modern English by Fowler, *Proverbs and Maxims of All Ages* by

82

Christy, *18,000 Words Often Mispronounced*, *Words—Their Use and Abuse* by Matthew.

Biography: "English Men of Letters" series, *Lives of the Poets* by Johnson, Boswell's *Johnson.*

Autobiography: Finney, George Fox, John Bunyan's *Grace Abounding,* memoirs of Grant and of Sherman.

Essays by Lamb, De Quincey, Swift, Macaulay, Bacon, Cicero, Washington Irving, Addison.

Fiction: Thackeray, Dickens, Hawthorne, and Scott; *Robinson Crusoe; Paul and Virginia* by St. Pierre.

Drama: Shakespeare, Goethe, Ibsen.

Bible—every translation, ancient and modern, is useful.

Parables: Trench, Bruce, Spurgeon, Guthrie.

Miracles: Trench, Lang.

Many preachers have found it a help in their preaching to have some special field in which they take a keen interest and in which they read deeply and widely. My own special interest is the American Civil War. My study of the great personalities of the period taking in the Civil War, civil, miltary, and in the pulpit, too, has given me a most interesting and profitable avocation. I think it is a good thing also if in his own particular field—that is, the Bible or church history—the minister gives special attention to one character, say David, or Peter, or Paul.

MAKING USE OF WHAT WE READ

What is the best plan to make profitable use of our reading? The minister should read with a pencil in his hand, and when a passage or a thought strikes him as something for future use, he should jot the word or the idea in the margin. For example, I have taken down from my shelves Minto's *Daniel Defoe,* in the "English Men of Letters" series. This is a series, edited by John Morley, through which I read early in my ministry. On the second page I see I have written in the margin, "Race pride." The reference is to Defoe's contempt for families that professed to have come over with the "Norman bastard" and his challenge to them to prove whether their ancestors were drummers or colonels. Leafing through the book, I find near the end a marginal notation, "Filial ingratitude." Speaking of the conduct of his son, Defoe writes: "It has been the injustice, unkindness, and, I must say, inhuman dealing of my own son which has both ruined my family, and in a word has broken my heart."

These passages struck me when I read the book years ago. Now, suppose I am to preach a sermon on the Fifth Commandment, "Honor thy father and thy mother," and I want an illustration on filial ingratitude. Although I have a fair memory, it is not likely that I should remember this passage in the life of Defoe; but I have it at hand in this way. When I had finished this book and the others in this long series, I noted the subjects jotted on the margins, with the book and the page for each, on file cards. Turning to this cabinet file, and looking at the card for "Ingratitude," I find this reference to Defoe—also one to the life of Jonathan Swift in the same series, one to *Gulliver's Travels,* and one to a sermon by Samuel Davies, the great Colonial preacher. Possibly, after all the years I might have retained some of these in my memory, but now, when I turn to these cards, I am able to refresh my memory in just a few minutes.

For poetical references I have a special file, and I mark all the books of poetry which I read as I go through them. Suppose I am going to preach a sermon on "Faith." I turn to my poetical file and find some of these references: Drinkwater, Wordsworth, Blake, with the appropriate pages noted. Suppose my subject is "The Fall of Man." Then I turn to that card and find the following: Emerson, Milton, Byron, pages so-and-so. If "Conscience" is my theme, I find the card "Conscience" and a note of Thomas Hood's "Eugene Aram's Dream." Thus, the fruits of reading are not thrown away. It is true that, just as a man will get good from a sermon at the time he hears it, although he may not remember a word or an idea of it twenty-four hours afterward, so one can get spiritual, mental, and moral help from a good book, although he may not remember anything in the book a short time after he has read it. But by use of a file a man can store special passages and incidents, and as the years go by he will accumulate a collection of valuable references to worth-while subjects. Out of his treasury, like the scribe instructed under the Kingdom of Heaven of whom our Lord spoke, he will be able to bring forth "things new and old."

OLD SERMONS

As a rule, the preacher takes a great distaste for his sermon after it has gone out of him. This is true especially of the sermons of the early years of one's ministry. As the years go by and his standards rise, as they ought to rise, the preacher will have a noble discontent—sometimes a contempt—for his sermons. Nevertheless, he should not throw them away, as he may be tempted to do. The eccentric but gifted preacher and poet Robert Hawker, vicar of Morwenstow, anxious to secure a good crop of turnips, fertilized his garden with the ashes of his burned sermons. The crop, however, was a total failure. Hawker attributed this to the admixture of a few of his grandfather's sermons, those being heterodox. But there is better use to make of old sermons than that. Let them be filed away in a sermon file with both text and subject references. For example, take a sermon on "Salvation by Faith." Let us say the sermon is on the text, "Believe on the Lord Jesus Christ, and thou shalt be saved." (Acts 16:31.) In the interleaved Bible—a most important part of the minister's equipment—will be written opposite verse 31 the numeral "100," referring to the sermon file. In the card index to the sermon file, under the subject "Salvation," the minister will find the reference to the sermon which he preached on that and other texts dealing with salvation by faith. Thus,

86

the minister himself builds up a sermonic library reference.

In using the interleaved Bible some preachers insert not only references to their own sermons and to other sermons on the text which they have in the library, but also to books, incidents, or personalities which they have in mind as opposite. The difficulty with this method is that one is apt to overload the pages of his interleaved Bible. Perhaps a better plan is to have in addition to the card index to books which the preacher has read—and in addition to his interleaved Bible references to his own and others' sermons—a general reference file.

Let the preacher by all means commence this general reference file early in his ministry. The first week is not too soon. Booklovers would not approve of what I have often done, but undoubtedly one of the most effective systems of quick and ready reference is to write on the margin or at the top or bottom of the page, then tear the page out and put it in the general file. There are many books that one will not read again, and from which, perhaps, he has got nothing to which he will refer again, save one or two incidents. Rather than let such a book gather dust on the shelves, it is better to tear out the page or two which are worth keeping and throw the book away.

Suppose our subject is "The Atonement." Looking in the general file under "Atonement," I find a copied paragraph from George Bernard Shaw's *Woman and Socialism* in which he expresses the enmity of the unregenerate mind toward the Atonement, and speaks of those who preach it and believe in it as persons "who actually make their religion center in the infamy of loading the guilt and punishment of all their sins on an innocent victim." This is a most important reference, not only because it expresses the natural man's distaste for the Atonement, but because it is an illustration of how what is of chief importance in the Christian faith can always be discovered and identified by the attacks that are made on it. I find a similar reference to Blatchford's *God and My Neighbor*. Speaking on the subject of substitution he says, "To forgive James because John has been unjustly flogged, would be to assert that because John was good, and because the master had acted unjustly, James deserved to be forgiven. This is not only contrary to reason and to justice, it is also very false sentiment." In this same file there are also a number of lines from Cowper dealing with the Lamb of God, the familiar words:

> I was a stricken deer that left the herd.
>
> . . . .
> There was I found by one who had himself
> Been hurt by th' archers.

Here, too, I find a reference to the life of Moody in which the evangelist states his creed as Isaiah 53. There is also a reference to a story in George Fox's *Journal* of how a friend went to Oliver Cromwell when Fox was languishing in a filthy dungeon in Lancashire and offered to take Fox's place if Cromwell would permit the exchange. The action so impressed Cromwell that he said to his council, "Which of you would do as much for me if I were in the same condition?" In this same file I find an outline of the views of one of the greatest writers on the Atonement, Turretini. There is also a poetical reference by Egbert Sanford:

> The sheep were safe
> Within the fold;
> The shepherd?—
> He was lost.

The file also has a reference to the words of David Brainerd on the moral and ethical value of faith in the Atonement: "I never got away from Jesus and Him crucified, and I found that when my people were gripped by this great evangelical doctrine of Christ and Him crucified, I had no need to give them instructions about morality. I found that one followed as sure and inevitable fruit of the other." Here is a clipping from a Roman Catholic paper under the heading "Whither Love Drove Mercy," which reads: "His infinite mercy suggested the Incarnation. Then His infinite love impelled the Eternal Son of God to go such lengths as He did in the Crucifixion to render an overwhelming reparation. Truly David was right when he foretold that it would be a plentiful redemption. (Ps. 129.)

These examples are sufficient to show the use which can be made of a general file in which the minister keeps pages torn from newspapers, books, and magazines, and his notes on incidents that have impressed him in his daily life.

CHOOSING TEXTS AND THEMES

It is highly important that the preacher should plan his work well ahead. When he preaches twice each Sunday, as I have done all through my ministry, then at least either the morning or the evening theme should be planned out long in advance. It is true that often the suggestion for a helpful sermon comes to the preacher only a few days before he has to preach. It may arise from some event in his pastoral experience, or from some significant happening in the world. For that reason, it is wise not to have too iron-clad a schedule. Even when the minister is preaching an announced series, he can sometimes interrupt it with a sermon on a special theme that has appealed to him, although, as a rule, it is not wise to interrupt a series.

In this connection it ought to be said that there is a great advantage in the minister's preaching regularly. Many ministers, especially in the first years of their ministry, when pressed with their work, or at loss for a sermon topic, are tempted to surrender their pulpits to some itinerant preacher, a member of a church board, or the president of a college who chances to come along. This seems to the pastor like a deliverance in the time of distress. But he makes a great mistake. In the first place, it is well to remember that although a visiting preacher may be an outstanding figure in the pastor's mind, he may be only a name to the parishioners—sometimes not even that. If a minister is happily placed, and there is a cordial relationship between pastor and people, the congregation will prefer to hear their own pastor. If a minister gets into the habit of vacating his pulpit every few weeks, the people will never know whether he is going to be there or not, and his work will suffer through interruptions. Regular and painstaking preparation for regular preaching is what counts in the minister's work.

SERMONS FROM LIFE

In selecting his themes the minister ought to see to it that the tone and accent of his preaching is varied. For example, when he has concluded a series of doctrinal sermons, the next series ought to be on, for example, Bible biographies, or on some of the problems of daily life—"Sermons from Life," as I have announced them in my own church. In my first pastorate I had an experience which suggested to me the plan of preaching such series. I had been asked by a businessman to call on his wife, from whom he had been separated because of financial difficulties. In the meantime she had secured employment out of town, and although he was now able to provide a home for her, she refused to go back to him. There was an intimation, also, that she had become attached to her employer. It was a difficult and delicate commission for me, but the man's distress was so great that I finally accepted it. His wife received me kindly, but made it plain that she had no intention of returning to her

91

husband. After I had prayer with her and was starting to leave, she said, "I believe that everyone has the right to be happy." That phrase followed me down the stairs and out to the street. It has followed me ever since. Some months afterward, a friend who knew of my fruitless errand, and of the dangerous situation, handed me a newspaper clipping which told of the woman's death under tragic circumstances. Immediately her parting words flashed back to me, "I believe that everyone has the right to be happy." That gave me the subject for the sermon, "Has Everyone the Right to be Happy?—The Right and the Wrong Idea of Happiness."

That was my first "Sermon from Life." Since then I have preached several series along that line. Each has been suggested by some incident of personal experience or pastoral work. A considerable period of time must elapse between such series, because such incidents do not occur daily. In such sermons there must be, of course, a complete anonymity and never in any way a betrayal of confidence.

There can be no objection to these sermons on personal experiences provided they center on and emerge from, not what the preacher himself has said or done, but what some other person has experienced. Although the psalmist and Paul preached out of their own experience and struck the chords of their own joy and hope and sorrow and transgression and overcoming faith, it is just as well for the preacher not to attempt to follow in their steps. The congregation are apt to weary of the personal life of its minister—what he saw or said, what his family did or said. The oft-exposed personality of the preacher is bound to grow dim and unimpressive. But there can be no objection to the use of a personal experience in another's life from which the preacher desires to draw his lesson. Even when the preacher does not make such an experience a sermon in itself, he can still use it for an illustration.

SERIAL PREACHING

How long a series should a preacher plan? I used to think five or six long enough. Sometimes the preacher can announce that many subjects, and then, if they work out well and popular interest is aroused, add to them. Frequently I have done that. I once preached fifteen sermons on a doctrinal series, "The Foundation Facts of the Christian Faith." I commenced with the Incarnation and ended with Heaven. In planning a long series like that, it may be wise to schedule it so that it will conclude on some special occasion, say Christmas or Easter. Thus the preacher works toward a climax. In the series on "Peter and His Lord" I preached twenty-one sermons, starting with Peter's call to be an apostle, and ending with his fifteen days with Paul at Jerusalem. In dealing with those fifteen days I had to use my imagination freely—what Peter said to Paul, and what Paul said to Peter. The advantage of a long series on a life such as that of Peter, or David, or Paul is that it compels one to continuous and consecutive Bible study. When the preacher finishes such a series, he feels that he knows every detail on his character's face.

There are also unusual sermon series which may be suggested by unusual experiences. For example, I have used memories of my many journeys in the footsteps of Paul to preach on the events of his life. In these sermons, laid in the Mediterranean world associated with Paul, I have dealt with almost every event in his life.

It is important that ministers should keep in touch with youth and their life and problems by preaching especially to young people from time to time. Every now and then sermons on friendship or friends are worth-while, such as:

> A Lost Friend—Samuel and Saul
> A Dangerous Friend—Amnon and Absalom
> A Young Woman and Her Boy Friend—Solomon and the Damsel of the Song of Songs
> A False Friend—Judas
> A Young Man and His Girl Friend—Samson
> A Friend Forever—Jesus

A series for young men and women which I found helpful was on "Life—Its Greatness and Its Peril," dealing with such topics as:

> Temptation—The Sword of David, or The Income from a Godly Youth
> Weak Moments—Esau
> Ambition—Absalom, or A Tomb Without a Tenant

Another series for young men and women in question form:

> What Shall I Dream?
> Whom Shall I Kill?
> Whom Shall I Obey?
> Whom Shall I Love?
> Whom Shall I Worship?

Another series was "For Her Sake," suggested by Herod Antipas' putting John the Baptist to death to please the wicked Herodias. Still another, "The Way of a Man with a Maid," was a study of men and women of the Bible in their relationship to one another: Adam and Eve, Ruth and Boaz, Jacob and Rachel, Joseph and Potiphar's wife, Samson and Delilah, David and Bathsheba, and, finally, Jesus and the woman who was a sinner.

Now and then a series on the Bible will be found profitable and will strengthen the hearts of the people. Nor should we forget the great characters of church history. I have been surprised to find how popular two series on "Great Preachers" were. A series on such characters as Augustine, John Huss, Savonarola, Martin Luther, John Calvin, John Knox, and other great reformers will give the preacher a highly profitable course of study, stir his mind, inspire his efforts, and do the people good.

SERMONS FROM THE PEOPLE

The preacher can often get sermon themes from his congregation. In the church calendar for a number of weeks I ran a notice asking the congregation to put down questions about the Bible and the Christian life which they would like to have answered. This resulted in a series of sermons on "Questions the People Are Asking." Naturally there were some questions which will have to wait for the answer until that day of which Jesus spoke when he said, "In that day ye shall ask me no questions." But there were some very helpful questions, such as: Can God bring blessing even out of our sins? Can we be certain of the validity of the Bible? Does the Bible teach the perseverance of the saints, but also the seeming contradiction that one can become an apostate? What about those who lived before Christ's day—did Christ die for them too? Was it necessary for Christ to die so as to make salvation sure for sinners? Why do bad men prosper? Can a soul that has been prayed over be lost? What is the "new birth"? What is "judgment to come"? Predestination—where does man's will come in? Why do you think so much of David? Forgiveness—can we forgive if forgiveness has not been sought?

At another time I asked the congregation to vote for "The Greatest Men and Women of the Bible." This gave me two series on the great men and the great women respectively. On the whole, the choices of the preacher and of the congregation were in agreement. I have also given the congregation an opportunity to vote on "The Great Texts of the Bible." At another time they were asked to put down subjects upon which they would like to hear a sermon. A request like that will bring in many foolish and trivial subjects, but also many that are well worth while.

In all his planning for the pulpit the preacher will do well to leave room for those particular and special inspirations, as it were, which come to him. Such themes not only arise from reading the Bible, or from personal experiences of the day, but come as if from nowhere—it may be as the preacher is lying quietly on his bed in the watches of the night, or as he sits meditating in his study, or even as he preaches in the pulpit. He can have a glad faith, too, concerning some of these themes, that they have been granted to him in a special way by the Holy Spirit, and he can go into the pulpit with an unusual assurance that he can say to his people what that patriot of the time of the judges said to the tyrant King of Moab before he slew him: "I have a message from God unto thee."

A series of sermons on "Prayer" is always timely and always helpful. Here are some of the topics I have used:

> Your Prayer for Others
> Your Unanswered Prayer
> Prayer for Deliverance
> Prayer and Temptation
> Prayer in Your Trouble
> Prayer and the Soul's Reserves

It will be profitable to take up some of the great prayers of the Bible, not necessarily stately and lengthy prayers, like Solomon's noble prayer at the dedication of the Temple, but prayers which come as a cry out of the depths of the soul—what we might call ejaculatory prayers—for example, Jacob's, "I will not let thee go, except thou bless me"; Balaam's, "Let me die the death of the righteous"; Elijah's, "O Lord, take away my life"; and David's, "My son, my son Absalom! would God I had died for thee." Dealing with prayers such as these, the preacher is sure to strike some of those strings that God hath strung in man's heart.

We should always bear in mind, too, the temptations, sorrows, and tragedies of human life. Men and women battle life daily. That means facing fear, temptation, anger, love, sex, remorse, loneliness, jealousy, doubt, and death.

PREACHING TO MEN

In my present church I have the great opportunity of speaking every Tuesday to a great company of businessmen at our Tuesday Noon Club. There is no gospel for man as distinguished from a gospel for women, no gospel for middle-aged people or aged people as distinguished from a gospel for youth; but there is an accent which is suitable for each different age and group. Here are some of the subjects of a series, "Great Soldiers of the Bible," which I delivered to these hundreds of men at the Tuesday Noon Club:

> Joshua, the Soldier After Whom Christ Was Named
> Saul, the Soldier Who Fell on His Own Sword
> David, the Soldier with the Broken Heart
> Gideon, the Soldier with the Broken Pitcher

The Soldier Who Preached at the Cross
Cornelius, the First Soldier to Come to Christ
The Last Conqueror—The White Horse and His
  Rider

Another year I took my subjects from road signs for
a series called "Along Life's Highway":

> Travel at Your Own Risk
> Detour
> Crossroads
> Stop, Look, Listen
> Soft Shoulders
> Forty Miles to ?

Another year the series was "I Met Twelve Men":

> The Man Who Was Too Busy
> The Man Who Used What He Had
> The Man Who Failed and Made Good
> The Man Revenge Ruined
> The Man Who Had a Grouch
> The Man Who Whispered
> The Man the Stars Fought
> The Man Who Lost What He Won
> The Man Who Wanted to Die

With these and other men of the Bible the preacher
can hold the mirror up to human nature. These men
are all real, and when one preaches on them he can
be sure that he is not as "one that beateth the air."

Recently I used at the Tuesday Noon Club, "The

Businessmen of the Bible," taking up most of the men who bought or sold:

> The Man Who Made a Corner in Real Estate (Lot)
> The Man Who Made a Corner in Cereals (Esau)
> The Man Who Made a Corner in Warehouses (the rich fool)
> The Man Who Made a Corner in Patriotism (Jeremiah and the field of Anathoth)
> The Man Who Made a Corner in Napkins (the talents)
> The Man Who Made a Corner on a Threshing Floor (David)
> The Man Who Made a Corner in Iron Chests (the hid treasure)
> The Man Who Made a Corner in Pearls (the pearl of great price)
> The Man Who Made a Corner in Sin (Judas)
> The Man Who Made a Corner in Souls (Jesus)

In announcing such a series as this, the biblical character or incident was not revealed until the sermon or address was being delivered. This has the advantage of arousing interest and curiosity in advance.

Sometimes it is a good plan to take one word in the Bible, but it must be a word that is worth preaching on—such as "Remember":

> Remember Now Thy Creator
> Son, Remember
> This Do in Remembrance of Me
> Eternity's Remember
> Remember Lot's Wife

100

APOLOGETIC PREACHING

When it comes to doctrinal preaching, it is hard to improve on the great and familiar statements of the Apostles' Creed. Gen. Robert Georges Nivelle, who at Verdun issued the famous command, "They shall not pass," left directions for his funeral: "I desire that the great affirmations of the Christian faith be spoken over my grave." In the Apostles' Creed we have the great affirmations of the Christian faith, the "things which are most surely believed among us." A series on these great doctrines will impress the people with the thought that "our religion is no bottomless mysticism, but is the Christian religion, and the Christian religion is founded squarely upon events like the death and Resurrection of our Lord."[1]

One hears it not infrequently said that the preacher's business is to proclaim the gospel, not to defend it. As a general proposition, this is true. But is there not a proclamation of the gospel in the very defense of it against doubt, misrepresentation, and unbelief? The Christian preacher, above all others, should be able and ready to give a reason for the faith that is in him, both to himself and to his people. I remember a saying of Dr. Francis L. Patton, of Princeton University and Princeton Theological Seminary, that if our faith cannot be vindicated at the bar of reason, it will be ruled out in the experience of life. Dr. David Burrell, then at the Marble Collegiate Church, New York,

---

[1]Dr. J. Gresham Machen.

and an occasional lecturer in homiletics at Princeton, impressed upon the students of my day the importance of logic in their preaching. Apologetic preaching of the right sort undoubtedly makes its appeal to most people. They like to see the foundations upon which their faith rests.

Very early in my ministry, in one of those London bookstalls in Paternoster Row, under the shadow of St. Paul's Cathedral, I picked up a little pamphlet which bore the title *Christianity and Common Sense*. I do not recall now the name of the author, and the pamphlet has long since disappeared from my library and its contents from my memory; but I am greatly indebted to whoever wrote that pamphlet, for it suggested to me a somewhat refreshing method of dealing with the truths which are revealed to mankind in the Christian faith. There are numerous defenses of Christianity on the basis of science. There are notable defenses on historical grounds. Great philosophers and logicians have defended the faith. But what is said in behalf of Christianity from the standpoint of common sense has a universal appeal, for all men are gifted with a certain degree of common sense and thus are qualified to pass upon the evidence. For example, take the scriptural doctrine of the fall of man. This is the most ridiculed, and perhaps the most maligned, of Christian doctrines. Yet, common sense, human history, and human experience are all on the side of the declared fact of the Bible, that human nature has suffered a catastrophe, and that the unity of man has

102

been broken by sin. This is attested by the universal sense of guilt.

> He knows a baseness in his blood
> At such strange war with something good,
> He may not do the thing he would.

In Scott's *The Pirate* one of the two sisters, in answer to the objection that human wisdom is worse than folly when applied to mysteries beyond its comprehension, says: "I think this doctrine only related to the mysteries of religion, which it is our duty to receive without investigation or doubt; but in things occurring in common life, as God has bestowed reason upon us, we cannot act wrong in employing it." But if this were true—that we can use our reason only in things occurring in common life, and not in matters of faith and revealed religion—then we should find ourselves in serious straits; for reason and common sense come from God, and his divine revelation of everlasting life through the gospel is addressed to a thinking and reasoning man.

Taking the title of that pamphlet *Christianity and Common Sense* as the title for a series of sermons, I took up, one by one, the great Christian doctrines, looking at them from the standpoint of common sense. I commenced with "Common Sense and Man" and ended with "Common Sense and Future Punishment and Rewards." My experience with such sermons and such series of sermons has left me in no doubt as to the value of such preaching and the drawing power of it. Let no one frighten us from such preaching by charging that we are proclaimers and not defenders, or that no one is ever argued into belief in Christian doctrine, or anything else that is good.

There are great doctrines which every preacher who wishes to declare the whole counsel of God ought to preach upon from time to time—the inspiration of the Scriptures, the Trinity, the Holy Spirit, the Incarnation, the Atonement, the Resurrection, the Second Advent, regeneration, future punishment, and heaven. The method followed by most Lutheran and Episcopal ministers of preaching through the church year and taking up great biblical and doctrinal themes Sabbath after Sabbath has the important advantage that it keeps the preacher from following too limited a course, to the neglect of important truths.

Doctrinal preaching furnishes an example of the sermon which is not immediately, although originally, suggested by a biblical text. The preacher selects his theme and then chooses a suitable text from the Bible. Suppose he is going to preach on the Judgment. There are many suitable texts, such as, "As he reasoned of righteousness, temperance, and judgment to come" (Acts 24:25), or, "We shall all stand before the judgment seat of Christ" (Rom. 14:10). Or suppose one is going to preach on the subject of predestination— one which I have discovered, during many years of preaching to congregations made up of all classes of

104

people, is a subject which always makes its appeal. There is no better text than, "Him, being delivered by the determinate counsel and foreknowledge of God, ye have taken, and by wicked hands have crucified and slain." (Acts 2:23.) In those words of Peter in his sermon on the day of Pentecost are the sovereign plan and determination of God and yet the freedom and responsibility of man in his acts. Or, suppose one is going to preach on "The Forgiveness of Sin." What better text is there than, "In whom we have redemption through his blood, the forgiveness of sins, according to the riches of his grace." (Eph. 1:7.) If one wants to preach on heaven, an unexcelled text is the familiar phrase from the Lord's Prayer, "As it is in heaven." Or you can use, "The powers of the world to come" (Heb. 6:5), or the words of Jesus, "And in the world to come" (Mark 10:30), or those haunting words of Paul, "The image of the heavenly" (I Cor. 15:49), or the interrogation of the psalmist, "Wilt thou show wonders to the dead?" (Ps. 88:10). The ease with which great texts of the Bible can be found for the great doctrines of the gospel is an indication of the importance of those doctrines.

STRANGE TEXTS

Again, there are texts which in themselves are striking and, in a way, strange. A preacher must be careful and restrained in the use of such texts, but now and then there will be a certain advantage in selecting a text which at once makes an impact on the mind of the hearer and arouses legitimate curiosity. I once preached a series of sermons on "Strange Texts But Grand Truths." They were as follows:

"Who told thee thou wast naked?" (Gen. 3:11)—Conscience

"There came out this calf" (Ex. 32:24)—Man's Alibi or Excuse for Sin

"A woman slew him" (Judg. 9:54)—The Fate of Many Men, and Some Preachers

"Michael the archangel, when contending with the devil he disputed about the body of Moses . . ." (Jude 9)—The Conflict for Good and Evil in Man's Soul

"Send us into the swine" (Mark 5:12)—The Downward Progress of Sin

"Break the bottle" (Jer. 19:10)—The Irrevocable in Life

"And cut off his great toes" (Judg. 1:6)—Retribution in Kind

"Alas, it was borrowed" (II Kings 6:5)—Life as a Stewardship (All we have is borrowed, and for it we must give an account.)

"Their sting is in their tails" (Rev. 9:10)—The End of Sin

REPEATING SERMONS

If the preacher is going to preach successfully from the Bible, he must always be working with the Bible. In my experience I have found the studies for the Wednesday night prayer meeting a very helpful preparation for future preaching. In these Wednes-

106

day night studies and discourses one breaks up, as it were, the soil for the sowing of the seed of the sermon that is to be. Indeed, that is true also of many sermons. A man may feel after he has preached on a certain text or theme that he has just touched the borders of the great continent of its thought, and that future sermons on the same text or theme will make a deeper and more powerful invasion.

This is the principal use to which a preacher can put his old sermons. If he has really worked and studied on some high biblical theme, he ought never to throw away his effort, for any consecrated work of that kind will be useful to him in a second, third, or even a fourth assault upon the citadel of truth. Nor should he hesitate to use the same text. Indeed, that is the honorable thing to do. When a minister boasts that he can preach the same sermon under the guise of a new text and no one will recognize it, that change of text is essentially dishonest, because by it he seeks to create the impression that he is preaching an altogether new and different sermon.

In my junior year at the seminary I went once to preach in a church in Newark, New Jersey. In the home where I was entertained I met a man who claimed to be a freethinker. He had been an ardent follower of one of the popular preachers in Chicago of a generation or more ago. One Sabbath the minister preached the same sermon he had preached before, but with a different text. The man regarded it as dishonorable, and sat under that preacher no longer.

It was one of the things he said had soured him on the church. Nor was he greatly to be blamed. If a sermon is worth repeating, and is preached with the true purpose, no preacher should be ashamed of the text which first suggested it to him.

But this has been something of a digression. My main purpose in speaking of preaching several times on the same text or the same subject is to show that the first time helps to prepare for the second, the second for the third, and so on. For myself, I have sometimes discovered that it was not until the third or fourth attempt that I was able to produce anything that seemed worthy of the text or profitable to the people.

GETTING AT THE SERMON

We have spoken of biblical reading, secular reading, and the different methods of keeping accessible the references which may be helpful. Now the time has come to get to work on the sermon. Let it be remembered, however, that this is not confined merely to those hours during the week before Sunday in which the preacher works on his subject. The preacher's whole life, his whole experience is, in a way, a preparation for the sermon, even though it may be an unconscious one. But now comes the actual and definite work of immediate preparation. How shall he go at it? Different men have different methods. All that one preacher can do is to explain his own methods, and say why they work best for him.

108

Let us say that the subject for Sunday morning is "Forgiveness." One of the most well-thumbed books in a minister's library ought to be his concordance. In it he will familiarize himself with those great and numerous passages of the Bible which deal with forgiveness. A good companion to the concordance is such a book as Nave's Topical Index. With the help of these two books the preacher can jot down those passages, incidents, and characters which deal with forgiveness in the Bible, and select those which he wishes to use.

The first thing the preacher must do is make up his mind just what the chief idea is that he wants to express. In speaking on forgiveness—divine forgiveness —the main thing he will want to set forth is the marvelous goodness, power, and wisdom of God in providing forgiveness for the sinner. Incidental to that will be the universal need of forgiveness. The gospel is the message—the "good tidings"—of the forgiveness of sin. That is the preacher's chief proposition, and with that he can persuade the people to accept forgiveness and live like forgiven men. "There is forgiveness with thee, that thou mayest be feared."

There are many ways in which the subject can be developed, but the preacher should certainly make an outline of what he wants to say. Sometimes this will grow as he reads and broods and meditates over the subject. Let him not be discouraged if it does not open up at once, or if his mind does not kindle to it. Remember what the psalmist said—although he probably meant it in a different connection—"While I was musing the fire burned." There is no worth-while subject to which the preacher's mind will not kindle if he thinks enough upon it and about it.

Let us suppose, then, that the theme and the text have been chosen, the proposition and a brief outline have been written out. It is true that the old-fashioned plan of outlining a sermon—introduction, proposition with heads 1, 2, and 3, and conclusion with appeal—cannot, of itself, make a worth-while or effective sermon. But it is also true that no good and effective sermon was ever hindered in its effectiveness by such a method of division and outline, but rather helped thereby. Such divisions show the people that the sermon has been carefully thought out and prepared. An outlined sermon will be a sermon, and not what so many alleged sermons are—mere rhapsodies.

Now let the preacher read everything worth while that he can on his subject. Let him turn to the theology books he used in his seminary days, his poetry file, his general file, his book file, and his own sermon index. It will not be possible to read everything to which reference has been made, but let him read as he has opportunity. In the reading his mind will begin to glow, and he will find himself reaching out and laying hold upon worth-while ideas. Then it is time to make a more lengthy sketch of the sermon. After a while he can go over the sketch and outline and put down additional thoughts. Very often I have made as many as four such sketches and outlines for one sermon.

At last the time comes to put the sermon into final form for the pulpit. One method is to take the last and fullest outline and use that as a guide and suggestion as the minister prepares to preach. Others will prefer to dictate the sermon in full, and others will type it or write it out. Thus the work of preparation is done. When the sermon has been completed, and the preacher works over it again, he will often hit upon new thoughts, ideas, or illustrations which he can use, although they may not be found in the completed manuscript. Ministers who have their sermons printed or published must write them out fully. Looking back through the experience of all these years, I should say that the most effective way is to make several outlines and prepare to preach from one of these. One danger to the minister in a fully written manuscript is that it tempts him either to read it or to reproduce it verbatim from memory in the pulpit. And what is that memorized reproduction but reading a sermon from the manuscript of the mind instead of from a page? But more along this line in the chapter on "Preaching Without Notes."

COMMENTARIES

So far I have said nothing about the use of commentaries. In the paragraphs above on books for the minister's library I have indicated some of the commentaries which I have found helpful. In my early ministry I made good use of the *Expositor's Bible* and Alexander McLaren's *Expositions of Holy Scrip-*

111

ture. I do not often refer to them now. The commentaries which I have found most helpful are: Ellicott's *Bible Commentary for Bible Students,* Matthew Henry's *Commentary, The Speaker's Bible,* Parker's *People's Bible, The Sermon Bible,* and Lange's *Commentary.* Too much consultation of commentaries is apt to have a serious effect on the preacher's resourcefulness, initiative, and originality. Let him remember that he has at least average intellect, common sense, understanding, and faith, and therefore has as much right to make a comment on the text of the Bible as anyone else.

What about using published sermons? There are some commentaries which fall in that category, such as *The Speaker's Bible* and Hastings' *Great Texts of the Bible.* These books are made up of sermon excerpts. It is good for the preacher to have some of the compilations of sermons by great preachers of the past. If a volume of sermons is worth while, the reference to these can be placed opposite the text in the interleaved Bible. Here again the preacher must be careful that he does not take his sermon from what some other preacher has said. If he gets into that habit, he not only runs the risk of plagiarism but may dry up the springs of his own imagination and reasoning.

What about books of illustrations? I remember that our church history professor at Princeton, Dr. John De Witt, giving us some counsel about preparation for preaching, said, incidentally, "And then you can throw your *Ten Thousand Illustrations* out of the window."

If I were asked to prescribe for the young preacher, I might well advise him not to buy books of illustrations during perhaps the first five years of his ministry. After that it is safe for him to do so—perhaps wise— for then he has more discrimination, more self-dependence, and can separate the wheat from the chaff in a book of illustrations.

Edmund Burke, the great stylist and orator, used to read passages from the prophecy of Isaiah before he made his stirring speeches in the House of Commons. He said that Isaiah's majestic sentences lifted up his mind and fused it with noble thoughts. That is a good plan for the preacher to follow. Passages from some of the great essayists, orators, poets, prophets, or apostles will calm his spirit and lift up his mind unto the hills of noble thought and aspiration.

What has been said thus far has had to do with what might be called the necessary mechanics and tools of sermonic preparation. We take for granted, of course, the minister's moral and spiritual preparation. The life that the minister leads during the week follows him up the stairs into the pulpit, and if that life has been worthy it will strengthen him and give him power and joy and liberty in utterance. One of the men of the French court once said to a famous court preacher, "Sire, your sermons terrify me, but your life reassures me."

It is possible—and frequently happens—that the preacher will go stale into the pulpit because he has overworked in his study. When one thinks of that, one

113

might be tempted to say, "Let me die the death of the righteous, and let my last end be like his!" Nevertheless, it is true that many a sermon is dull and many a preacher is lifeless in the pulpit because he has been too shut off from social intercourse and has not refreshed his spirit with the sunlight of life. Thus it is that faithful pastoral work is in itself one of the most helpful and important parts of sermon preparation. From pastoral experiences the preacher speaks not as an academician, but as one who is touched with a feeling for the infirmities, sorrows, trials, and hopes of mankind.

Every preacher will know and understand that some of his best work will be done altogether apart from the careful and painstaking plans and methods which I have just outlined. As he is walking along the street, listening to conversation, or lying awake in the watches of the night, his theme, text, and divisions will come to him, and he will outline his sermon and write it without opening a book, perhaps not even the Bible. But that happens because in the course of his work he has been faithful in his study of the Bible and has given himself, as Paul advised Timothy, "to reading."

Every thoughtful and hard-working preacher runs the risk of being tempted into some bypath of peculiarity in his choice or development of theme. He may become so interested himself in that particular by-product of truth that he will not realize that it fails to grip the people, or that it is not what they need.

One of the best ways to avoid this is to be certain that there is a variety of themes and subjects, that the great doctrines of the gospel are dealt with, and that the great incidents and characters of the Scriptures are not neglected.

When Charles Francis Adams, America's great ambassador to Britain during the Civil War, was in London, he went one day to hear Spurgeon preach, and recorded his impressions: "There was no characteristic thought or novel reasoning. His power consisted in sympathy with the current of human feeling in all ages on that solemn topic of Moral Responsibility to a Higher Power both here and hereafter." It is evident from this comment, and also from the reading of Spurgeon's sermons, that he did not wander aside into some of those bypaths which often tempt ministers from the broad avenues of Christian truth, but kept his emphasis upon the grand affirmations of the Christian faith about God, the soul, salvation, sin, judgment, and the life to come.

PREPARING FOR PUBLIC PRAYER

Perhaps the most neglected part of the service in most nonliturgical churches is the pulpit prayer. The minister spends all his time and energy in preparing his sermons and is apt to neglect altogether the preparation for the high office of public prayer. One of the things which impressed me in the letters received from those who listened to our services over the radio was the number of people who testified to the help they had found in the pulpit prayer. Sometimes the preacher will be able to do for some soul in his prayer what he cannot do in his preaching. Henry Ward Beecher, whose pulpit prayers have been recorded together with his sermons, was as remarkable in one as in the other. Of all the prayers which I have read, Beecher's are the ones which I would commend to the minister for study and inspiration. Beecher's great nature overflowed in an apparently exhaustless fountain of intercession and supplication. Speaking on this aspect of the minister's work, Beecher said:

I think the most sacred function of the Christian ministry is praying. I can bear this witness that never in the study in the most absorbed moments, never on the street in those chance inspirations that everybody is subject to when I am lifted up highest, never in any company where friends are the sweetest and dearest, never in any circumstances in life is there anything to me so touching as when I stand in ordinary good health before my great congregation to pray for them. Hundreds and hundreds of times as I rose to pray and glanced at the congregation, I could not keep back the tears. There came to my mind such a sense of their wants, there were so many hidden sorrows, there were so many weights and burdens, there were so many doubts, there were so many states of weakness, there were so many dangers, so many perils, there were such histories, not world histories, but eternal world histories.

I had such a sense of compassion for them, my soul longed for them, that it seemed to me that I could scarcely open my mouth to speak for them. And when I take my

116

people and carry them before God and plead for them, I never plead for myself as I do for them—I never could. There is no time that I get so far into heaven. I can see my mother there. I see again my little children. I walk again arm in arm with those who have been my companions and co-workers. I forget the body. I live in the spirit, and it seems as if God permitted me to lay my hand on the very Tree of Life and to shake down from it both leaves and fruit for the healing of my people, and it is better than a sermon; it is better than an exhortation.

Perhaps the great majority of ministers use extemporaneous prayer. From reading Beecher's prayers, I rather judge it was so with him. But there are few Beechers. Most ministers who rely upon the moment, and whose prayers are purely extempore, will repeat themselves Sunday after Sunday. Their prayers are stereotyped, but without the advantage of the noble language of the liturgies. One of the notable ministers of the First Presbyterian Church, Pittsburgh, was Dr. Francis Herron. He was a mighty power in the city and in the denomination. But his power lay in his upright Christian character and piety rather than in his genius or talent. His public prayers were always the same. Late-comers arriving during the long prayer would irreverently ask those standing about the door, "Has he got to the dry bones yet?" The reply would tell them how long they had to stand, for the prayer was always the same. The reference, of course, was to the "dry bones" of Ezekiel's vision.

However, monotonous and similiar as Dr. Herron's prayers were, he was always praying for the shaking of the dry bones and the coming of a revival. And it came!

Perhaps the best method is to give careful thought to the subject matter of public prayer. If the preacher prepares himself to speak to the people on Sunday, why should he not also prepare himself when he speaks to God in behalf of the people and his own soul? In such preparation the preacher can follow, if he wishes to do so—although even in that there is danger of monotony—the classical order of adoration, thanksgiving, confession, supplication, and intercession. Following such an order will at least suggest to the preacher certain definite things which he desires to mention in his petitions. Some have found it helpful to keep a folder for prayer notes—the thoughts and desires that come during the week—and from these select certain topics. The range covered by the average minister's prayer is usually very limited, and the reason is that he has made little preparation. In order to avoid mere memoriter verbatim reproduction of some prayer that he has written, the minister should put down just a skeleton outline of the prayer he desires to offer. Then in the inspiration of the sacred environment and the sacred hour he will be able to frame suitable language and clothe his thoughts in appropriate words.

The preacher ought to remember that the hymnal is really a compilation of prayers, and hence that one of the best preparations for public prayer is the reading of the hymnbook. I do not believe that the average person in a congregation likes to hear a minister quote verses of hymns in his prayer, no matter how beautiful and how familiar those verses may be. The almost inevitable effect is to create the impression that the preacher is reciting to the people instead of praying to God. But great hymns can be used in public prayer in another way. Let the preacher take one of the noble hymns, especially those not so much of adoration and praise, as of supplication, and then put into prose the petitions of the different verses. He is fairly certain, then, to make a prayer that will do the people good, and which is not just a monotonous series of "O Lord, bless this," or "O Lord, bless that." Still better, let the preacher weave the noble language of the Scriptures into his prayers. All those who heard my father in the pulpit spoke of him as a man unusually gifted in prayer, and I remember distinctly the uplifting influence of his public prayers, and also his prayers at the family altar. What I remember most about them is the number of beautiful passages from the prophets, especially Isaiah, which he wove into his petitions.

The one thing above all else to avoid is seeming to deliver a speech or an oration to the Almighty. One of the most eloquent of the Colonial preachers was Samuel Davies. Men sometimes wondered that one who was so forceful as a preacher seemed very limited in his prayers. The reason was that his sense of the divine Presence filled him with such awe, humility, and self-abasement that his apparent hesitancy made people think he was at a loss for expression. Some of his brethren once told him that he hardly appeared to be the same man in addressing the Throne of Grace as in the delivery of his sermons. To this Davies answered, "God forbid that I should play the orator before my Maker, whatever I may do before my fellow worms of the dust."

On occasions the preacher can, before commencing his prayer, ask the people to pray for some particular thing near to their hearts. This will help put them in a receptive and devotional mood. Once in a famous London church I heard the minister in his public prayer enumerate the different objects for which he was going to pray, and ask the people to pray silently for each one, after which he made an audible prayer. Impressive as this was, I felt that it had a tendency to take away from the reverence and beauty of prayer.

Whatever method the preacher pursues—and I have indicated that which calls for the most labor and preparation—he must try to forget himself in his public prayers. He must forget his own failures, weaknesses, and coldness of heart. He must always remember that he is praying, not for himself alone, but for hundreds of souls, and that it is his high privilege and office to lead them unto the mercy seat.

IV

BIBLE BIOGRAPHICAL PREACHING

GOD IS THE GREAT, ORIGINAL, AND CONTINUAL BIO-
graphical preacher. In John's Gospel we read, "In the
beginning was the Word, and the Word was with God,
and the Word was God. . . . And the Word was made
flesh, and dwelt among us, (and we beheld his glory,
the glory as of the only begotten of the father), full
of grace and truth." And in Paul's Second Epistle to
the Corinthians we read: "God, who commanded the
light to shine out of darkness, hath shined in our
hearts, to give the light of the knowledge of the glory
of God in the face of Jesus Christ." God did not
reveal himself in abstract truth, but in a life—in the
life of his son Jesus Christ. The goal of every earnest
preacher is to make the word which he proclaims become flesh, and, as it were, dwell among men. That
is the great purpose of biographical preaching. The
truth is revealed in the personalities of the Bible.

Contorini Fleming once wrote, "Read no history;
nothing but biography, for that is life without theory."
The Bible is the supreme book on human personality.
Great novelists like Hugo, and Hawthorne, and Dickens strive to give the reader clear sketches of personalities. That is what the Bible does. From Adam in

121

Genesis to Satan in the Apocalypse, its portraits are unforgettable. Man is the great wonder. Augustine wrote how men wander over the earth and wonder at the rivers and the mountains and the sea and the stars, while all the time man himself is the great wonder. In every respect man is "fearfully and wonderfully made." How fearful and how wonderful are man's terrible and glorious capacities and possibilities, the Bible, above all books, tells us. It is said that every man's life contains sufficient material for a great novel. So in every character depicted in the Bible there is material for a great sermon.

Not only is the Bible the greatest of biographers, but a large portion of it consists of biography. That will be seen by an examination of its books. Genesis is largely biography—the stories of Adam and Eve, of Noah, Abraham, Isaac, Jacob, Esau, and Joseph. Exodus, Numbers, and Deuteronomy are not only narrative but biographies, for in those books we have the lives of Pharaoh, Moses, Aaron, Hur, Miriam, Balaam, and Joshua. The book of Joshua is, in a sense, the biography of that great soldier. Judges gives us the biographies of the judges, such as Gideon, Samson, Abimelech, and Jephthah. The book of Ruth is a gem of biography. The two books of Samuel give us the biographies of Samuel, Saul, David, and Jonathan. Kings and Chronicles give us the biographies of the kings of Judah and Israel, from Solomon to Jehoiachin. Large portions of Ezra and Nehemiah are biographical. Esther is one of the masterpieces of biography, with its unforgettable sketches of Ahasuerus, Vashti, Haman, Mordecai, and Esther. What is the book of Job but the biography of Job's soul? Large portions of the Psalms are biographical in the sense that they are autobiographical. In a certain sense Ecclesiastes is autobiographical. So is the Song of Solomon. Isaiah has many biographical passages, such as its brief sketch of the prophet himself, and the very full and interesting portrayal of the good King Hezekiah. Jeremiah, much more than the book of Isaiah, is biographical. Ezekiel gives us a portrait of that great prophet, the visions and dreams which he experienced, the messages which he delivered, and the judgments which he acted out as if in a drama. Daniel is one of the greatest of biographies. The minor prophets provide splendid biographical passages, such as the marriage of Hosea to the faithless Gomer. Jonah is a brief but powerful biography.

When we turn to the New Testament, we have in the four Gospels the biographies of Jesus. The Acts of the Apostles gives us sketches of Peter, John, and Herod, but it is in large part the biography of Paul. The letters to the Corinthians and to the Galatians have important biographical portions, and without those sketches our knowledge of Paul would be much less than it is. Philippians, Thessalonians, and the two epistles to Timothy have many biographical pages dealing with Paul and his associates. Philemon is a one-chapter masterpiece of autobiography which lets us into the heart of Paul. In the Apocalypse the things that one best remembers, perhaps, are what is said about John in his captivity, about the Lamb of God, the two faithful witnesses, the woman clothed with the sun, and her child, the beast, the false prophet, and the dragon.

The Bible contains what we might call different types of biographies. There are, first of all, those of the major characters, such as Abraham, Isaac, Jacob, Moses, Joshua, Joseph, Samuel, David, Solomon, Saul, Elijah, Jeremiah, and Jonah. Then there are what we might term the biographies of lesser great men, such as Josiah, Ezra, Nehemiah, Jonathan, Barnabas, and Timothy. There are others we might describe as thumbnail sketches. They are sometimes just an intimation of a biography—Jabez, who was more honorable than his brethren; the poor wise man who saved a city and was forgotten; those two young kings, Jehoram, who departed without being desired, and Abijah, of whom it is written, "They buried him; and all Israel mourned for him"; the man of God who cried against Jeroboam's altar at Bethel and was slain by the lion; the young man of the Gospels who fled naked in Gethsemane; Demas, who forsook Paul; Felix, who trembled; Gehazi, a leper white as snow; Herod, who was eaten of worms; Onesimus, the fugitive slave; and Onesiphorus, who was not ashamed of Paul's chains. Some of these characters, sketched with just a single stroke, stir the curiosity of the preacher and give a splendid opportunity for the play of his imagination.

In the field of child biography there are little girls such as Jephthah's daughter; Rhoda, who kept Peter waiting at the door; the captive maid who told Naaman of Elisha; Miriam, who outwitted Pharaoh; the girl of the Gospels who had an evil spirit; and the daughter of Jairus. Among the boys of the Bible are Samuel, David, the good King Josiah, the nephew of Paul, and Jesus in his youth.

The parables are largely biographical. That is why we remember them so well—the two men and their two houses, the two debtors, the unforgiving debtor, the good Samaritan, the friend at midnight, the unjust judge, the rich fool, the prodigal son, the unjust steward, Dives and Lazarus, the two sons, the Pharisee and the publican. The power and charm of these parables lies in their revealing insight into human nature. What a wide field there is for biographical preaching, too, in great autobiographical books such as Ecclesiastes, Job, and certain of the psalms. Nor can we forget the women of the Bible—Sarah, Rebekah, Rachel, Hannah, Bathsheba, Abigail, Esther, Lot's wife, Delilah, the woman of Samaria, the Shunammite woman, Mary and Martha, the woman who was a sinner, and the virtuous woman of the book of Proverbs.

Plutarch, the great master of biography, compares and contrasts forty-six Greek and Roman characters. He sketches them in pairs and draws his comparisons between them. Some of the characters of the Old and New Testaments lend themselves to similar treatment.

This has the added advantage of novelty. For example, take David and Peter. Both owed much to friendship; both were men of the heart; both, although greatly sinning, were in a sense men after God's own heart. Both are monuments to the power of temptation, and warn us, "Let him that thinketh he standeth take heed lest he fall." Both show us how no religious office, no familiarity with religious things, no association with religious people are in themselves a guarantee against temptation and sin. Another interesting comparison is Pharaoh and Herod the Great. Both were kings, and both men of great ability and energy. Both were great builders—Pharaoh, of the colossal treasure cities; Herod, of the ivory palace at Jericho and the rebuilt Temple. But both were also men of great cruelty. Pharaoh ordered the massacre of the male infants of a whole nation, and Herod caused the murder of the infants of Bethlehem and the surrounding country. Both men strove in vain to defeat the plan and purpose of God, Pharaoh by casting the male children into the Nile, Herod by the slaughter of the innocents. Both were found to be "fighting against God." But the decree of Herod and the decree of Pharaoh were both set aside by the decree of God. At the beginning of these two great epochs in the history of redemption, in these two fragments of divine providence, we see the purpose of God going invincibly forward to its fulfillment, and the vain attempt of man to frustrate it or turn it aside.

Another interesting comparison is that between

126

Balaam and Judas. They are the dark shadows of the Old and New Testaments. Both were men of superior talents and opportunities. Balaam was a genius, and Judas must have had high capacity to have been chosen as one of the Twelve. Both of them sinned against their opportunity. Both of them went to their doom in spite of repeated warnings. Balaam rushed through the barrier of his own conscience and past the sword of the angel. Judas was warned more than once by Jesus. Both tampered with conscience, and the light that was in them became darkness. Both were men slain by avarice. For Balak's gold Balaam seduced Israel to sin; for thirty pieces of silver Judas betrayed Christ. Both Judas and Balaam tell us that good environment, high responsibility, and spiritual ambition cannot, of themselves, save a man from sin and shipwreck unless he also sets himself to do the will of God. In *Pilgrim's Progress*, the pilgrim saw a door to hell close to the gate to heaven. So, close to the highest spiritual privileges, offices, and desires, there may be a door that opens into hell.

Two of the greatest men of the Bible—one of the Old Testament and one of the New—were Elijah and John the Baptist. Both were children of the desert and of solitude. They were alike in their dress. Elijah was a hairy man, with a girdle of leather about his loins. John the Baptist was clothed with camel's hair and a girdle of skin. Both were given messages of judgment and denunciation, and in the discharge of their commissions they displayed superb courage. Elijah denounced Ahab and Jezebel; John the Baptist flayed the scribes and the Pharisees and rebuked Herod for his adulterous union. Both were pursued by the enmity of a wicked woman, one by Jezebel, the other by Herodias. Both were great and sublime in the faith, and yet both suffered a temporary eclipse of faith and passed under the cloud of doubt—Elijah when he fell on his face beneath the juniper tree, and John the Baptist when he sent from his dungeon that message of doubt to Jesus, "Art thou he that should come? or look we for another?" Both men are immortal in their influence, Elijah or John the Baptist—either name is like a conquering army with banners.

Among the advantages of preaching on Bible characters are the following: First of all, as we have seen, the sermon is bound to be real and true to life. A man may be preaching on a Bedouin chieftain like Abraham and Jacob, but what he can say about them will apply just as well to the businessman who sits behind a mahogany desk in his office, for human nature is the same the world over. Or a man may be preaching on the fall of David, and what he says about temptation and passion and conscience and retribution can just as much concern a modern professional man.

Another advantage of preaching on Bible characters is that the sermon will have a freshness about it. It is no longer wise to take for granted any wide degree of knowledge concerning the Bible. I preached once on Abigail, whose speech to David, restraining him from his vengeance upon Nabal, is perhaps the second most eloquent speech in the Bible—the first, I should say, being that of Judah when he pleaded with Joseph not to hold Benjamin as a hostage. At the close of the service a woman told me she had never known there was such a story in the Bible. Even when the story is most familiar, it still makes its appeal. I remember hearing an Anglican bishop preach on David and Goliath. The fact that the theme was so familiar only added to my interest in the sermon. In that respect, it is like a congregation or an audience listening to familiar and well-loved music. Biblical biography touches every chord in the human heart. A prominent shipbuilder once said to me, "My minister is an able and consecrated man and preaches carefully prepared sermons, but I would much prefer that he would take one of the old narratives of the Bible, or one of the Bible characters, and build his sermon around that narrative or that character."

Still another important advantage of preaching on biblical characters is that what the preacher says will be remembered. When I was in the seminary, our distinguished president, Dr. Francis L. Patton, gave us lectures in ethics. The only one of all those lectures that is still fresh in my mind is a brief biographical sketch of Spinoza. Dr. Patton told us the facts of his life, how he was a Portuguese Jew, how he was excommunicated from the synagogue, how he supported himself by grinding and polishing lenses for spectacles, telescopes, and microscopes; also the circumstances of his death. The biographical facts remain;

the philosophical teachings are gone. In that popular book *The Raft,* which tells of the experiences of some airmen who came down in the Pacific, it was brought out that none of them could remember anything that the chaplains had preached. But some of the men had attended Sunday School, and they were able to recall the great stories of the Bible. In the long and lonely days and nights of drifting on the vast Pacific, these men comforted one another with those great stories.

Again, one of the best ways in which to preach doctrinal sermons, or to drive home personal and ethical truths, is to use characters of the Bible. Many a preacher, after wandering into the far country and feeding his people and himself on the husks which the swine did eat, has returned again to the Bible and been surprised to discover how new, fresh, and powerful it is. In preaching on Bible characters the preacher has no need to go far afield for his illustrations. The great stories illustrate themselves.

DIFFERENT METHODS OF TREATMENT

One way is to relate the story of a biblical character and make the points of the sermon as you go through the story. Here are a few examples of that method:

Daniel: (*a*) Daniel's youth and how he fitted himself for his great career by a moral stand. He purposed in his heart that he would not defile himself with the king's meat. (*b*) Daniel's manhood. His courage and fidelity in his prayers to God and his deliverance out of the lion's den. (c) Daniel's honor and reward. God never forgets those who honor him.

Abraham: (a) His call—through him and the Jews all nations to be blessed. "Thou shalt be a blessing." Every man can be a blessing to the world. (b) Abraham's friendship with God and his power as an interceder. (c) Abraham's sin in passing his wife off as his sister. How he fell where he was strong in his faith. How others fall in that same way. (d) The great trial of his faith in the offering up of Isaac. How his faith was vindicated. How God tries men today to see if they will trust in him.

Elijah: (a) The comfort and kindness of God which Elijah ministered to others, notably in the case of the widow of Zarephath. (b) Elijah as a minister of the judgments of God upon Ahab and Jezebel. Elijah the symbol of judgment. "Elijah is here." Always we can paraphrase that, "The God of judgment is here." (c) The discouraged Elijah, and how God ministered to him. (d) The power of prayer. Elijah and the drought and the rain. (e) Elijah and the Transfiguration. The certainty and the glory of the future life.

Samuel: (a) A godly mother. (b) The call of God and a converted child. (c) Samuel magnificent in adversity. (d) The posthumous influence of Samuel, and of all good men. Saul's request of the witch of Endor, "Bring me up Samuel."

Jacob: (a) Jacob's sin of deceit against his father and his brother Esau. His exile. How sin finds us out.

(*b*) Jacob the lover. Jacob and Rachel. (*c*) Jacob regenerated. The midnight struggle with the angel.

David: (*a*) David as a man after God's heart. His thankfulness, his filial piety, his magnanimity, his affection, his devotion. (*b*) David as a man against God's heart. David's temptation and fall. The displeasure of God. (*c*) David's conviction and repentance. The sermon on the ewe lamb by Nathan. How David warns us that religious associations and religious desires are not sufficient to keep the soul from sin. How he tells us that sin has the power to blind a man to his own sin, while he denounces sin in others. How he shows us that sin can be forgiven, and yet that the way of the transgressor is hard. How he preaches on the text, "Be sure your sin will find you out." How David's repentance still teaches God's ways to transgressors.

Joseph: (*a*) The dreams of Joseph. Dreamers are the achievers. (*b*) Joseph resisting temptation, "How then can I do this great wickedness, and sin against God?" (*c*) Joseph in the dungeon. Yet God was with him in the dungeon, as he is with every faithful soul. (*d*) Joseph honored and exalted. His magnanimity, his affection, and his forgiveness of his brethren. In this respect, Joseph is the most Christlike man in the Old Testament.

Moses, the man of three mountains: (*a*) The mountain of revelation. Moses and the Ten Commandments. Will man live by his own wisdom and bread, or by the word of God? (*b*) The mountain of intercession.

Moses praying for the people, when Israel battled with the Amalekites. As long as he held his rod aloft, Israel prevailed. The Church prevails by her prayers. The prayer of Moses for the people after the sin of the golden calf. His compassion and pity. (c) The mountain of disappointment, Mount Pisgah. Moses forbidden to enter the Promised Land. Yet centuries later he stands in glory on the mount with Elijah when Christ was transfigured. God's disappointments in the end will prove to be our blessings.

Another method is to tell the story and then make the points of the sermon. The following are examples of this method:

Balaam: (a) Tampering with conscience. (b) No man unwarned of his fall. (c) The insufficiency of emotion and religious desires without perseverance and endurance to the end.

The woman of Samaria: (a) How Christ satisfies the soul. (b) The divine in every soul. (c) The passing opportunity, "If thou hadst known!"

Elisha and the Shunammite woman: (a) Noble motherhood. (b) The thought of a mother in the time of temptation. (c) The comfort of a mother, and a mother's faith in the time of sin. "Carry him to his mother."

Rahab the harlot: (a) Her decision for God and God's people. (b) Faith saved her. Faith in Christ saves the sinner.

Lot's wife: (a) Halfway Christians. "For where your treasure is, there will your heart be also." (b)

133

The dangerous power of a look. (c) The appeal of the angels.

Abigail, the woman who married the wrong man: (a) A woman unsoured by adversity. (b) God's providence in our lives, "Bound in the bundle of life." (c) The regrets we have missed, and those we *can* miss if we listen to the pleading of the Holy Spirit.

Some of the characters of the Bible lend themselves to treatment in a series of sermons. One of the most helpful would be a series on David. You might call it "Chords from David's Harp":

David Chosen
David and the Evil Spirit
David and the Giant
David and Jonathan
David and Saul
David and Bathsheba—His Sin and Repentance
David and Absalom
David and the Census
David and Doeg
David and the Well of Bethlehem
David and the Sword of Goliath
David and Abigail

Another profitable series would be one on Peter:

Peter's Call
Peter's Confession
Peter Walking on the Sea
Christ's Prayer for Peter
Peter's Fall

134

Peter's Tears
Peter Restored
Peter's Shadow
Peter at the Gate Beautiful
Peter in Prison

The great doctrines of the Bible and of the gospel ought to be taught and proclaimed from the pulpit. One of the most acceptable and effective ways in which this can be done is through doctrinal preaching that is also biographical. For example, take "Repentance." Instead of speaking of repentance in the abstract, preach on it in the concrete—cite well-known men and show how repentance occurred in their lives. A sermon on repentance might thus have in it: (*a*) David's repentance, (*b*) Peter's repentance, and (*c*) the thief's repentance.

Again, one might preach a series of sermons on "Men Who Repented." It could include Manasseh, the aged and wicked king of Judah, Saul (or false repentance), David, Job, Peter, the penitent thief.

If a preacher is going to speak on "conversion," the subject is best explained and illustrated by examples of actual conversions. I find that I once preached on the following characters in a series on "Great Conversions."

Cornelius—The Good Man Who Became a Christian Man
The Ethiopian Eunuch—The Royal Treasurer Who Found True Treasure

135

The Philippian Jailer—The Man Whom an Earth-
quake Brought to Christ
Paul—The Greatest Foe Becomes the Greatest
Friend
The Penitent Thief—The Thief Who Stole Heaven

Outside scriptural figures, an interesting and helpful series on great conversions might include Augustine, Peter Waldo, Luther, Bunyan, John Newton, and
Colonel Gardiner. One sermon on conversion might
include three or four of the notable instances of conversion in the Bible, such as Peter, Cornelius, the
Philippian jailer, and the Ethiopian eunuch.

Take the great theme of "Forgiveness." Instead of
talking about forgiveness, call your sermon "Men Who
Were Forgiven." Such a sermon could take in the
woman who was a sinner, Paul, the penitent thief, and
Peter.

Then there is the great theme—often neglected by
the preacher—"Divine Providence," both in individual lives and in history. There are two characters
in the Bible who, perhaps above all others, offer a
splendid foundation for a sermon on providence. One
of these is Joseph, whose trials and sufferings were
overruled by God for the salvation of Israel and for
the carrying out of God's great plan through his chosen
people. The splendid text for such a sermon is, "But as
for you, ye thought evil against me; but God meant it
unto good." (Gen. 50:20.) The second character is
Esther. For preaching on God in history there is no

136

book in the Bible and no character comparable to Esther. This book does not have the name of God in it, and yet no other book in the Bible gives us such a lesson of God's place in history. The most fitting text for such a sermon would be, "On that night could not the king sleep." (Esther 6:1.) With that text one can tell the whole story of Esther—how, through such an apparently chance event as the insomnia of an Oriental despot, the wicked plot to destroy Israel was frustrated.

Another great theme for the preacher is "Temptation." Here the preacher is never as one that beateth the air. Instead of speaking about temptation in the abstract, illustrate it by the real temptations that assailed men in the Bible, such as the temptations of Joseph, Samson, David, and Peter. On this subject one could also preach a series of sermons on the men of the Bible who said No, that is, No to temptation— Joseph, Nehemiah, Daniel, Moses, Vashti, the Hebrew lads, and Jesus. The circumstances of these various temptations can be related with stirring effect.

The subject of "Dreams" is one which appeals particularly to youth. Here is such a series:

The Angel's Ladder—Jacob's Dream
The Eleven Stars—Joseph's Dream
Life's Choice—Solomon's Dream
The Great Image—Nebuchadnezzar's Dream
A Woman's Premonition—Pilate's Wife's Dream
The Man from Macedonia—Paul's Dream

It is a good thing now and then for the minister to preach on the subject of "Anger," the most foolish sin, and one of the most dangerous. Here he might make use of Balaam beating his ass, Jonah and his gourd, Naaman and Elisha, and the Elder Brother.

Another dangerous sin is jealousy. Here one can speak of Saul, that character who always fascinates, thrills, and saddens. Slander is another dreadful sin. Preaching a sermon on slander, the preacher can tell how Doeg slandered David to Saul, or how Gashmu and his associates slandered Nehemiah. The text for that sermon would be, "And Gashmu saith it." (Neh. 6:6.)

One of the most common sins in the world is ingratitude. There is no better text for a sermon on this sin than, "Yet did not the chief butler remember Joseph, but forgat him." (Gen. 40:23.) Another text for that subject comes from the story of Jesus and the ten lepers whom he healed—"Where are the nine?" (Luke 17:17.) It is a natural thing to speak on gratitude at the same time that one is preaching on ingratitude. There are two beautiful instances of gratitude related in the Bible. One is in the life of David. When David had at last reached the throne and desired to prove his gratitude to God, he showed the kindness of God to the lame son of his old friend Jonathan. The other instance is from the history of Saul. When he had fallen in battle, and the Philistines had nailed his headless body as a ghastly trophy to the walls of Bethshan, the men of Jabesh-gilead, who had been rescued by Saul out of the hand of the Ammonites, risked their lives at night to rescue Saul's body and give it decent sepulture.

An always timely subject for the preacher and his people is "Opportunity." There are many texts which can be used, perhaps none better than the familiar, "Now is the accepted time." (II Cor. 6:2.) This subject can be well presented and illustrated, particularly on the side of lost opportunity as follows: (a) Esau. After having sold his birthright for a mess of pottage, and having been cheated out of the blessing that belonged to the first-born by Jacob, Esau could find "no place of repentance, though he sought it carefully with tears." One must be careful, however, to point out that it is not the impossibility of repentance from sin which is spoken of in that verse in Hebrews, but the impossibility of getting back the lost blessing. That was irrecoverable. (b) The lost prisoner. The parable of the son of the prophets who condemned Ahab for his foolish leniency toward Benhadad, the defeated king of Syria. (c) Christ and the sleeping disciples in Gethsemane. "Sleep on now, and take your rest." The opportunity to watch with Christ in his agony was forever gone. They could witness for him, preach for him, suffer for him, and die for him; but that Gethsemane opportunity was gone forever. (d) The foolish virgins and the shut door. The infinite pathos of the door that is closed against the soul. Such illustrations as these can be co-ordinated into one sermon, or used individually in a series.

"Adversity" is a theme that always comes close to human need and experience. Sooner or later, all men drink of that cup. The story of Job is the greatest sermon on that subject. Perhaps the most effective way to preach on Job is first of all to tell his story: (a) The first test—loss of his property and his family. (b) The second test—affliction of his body. (c) The third test—the arraignment of Job by his three friends and the charge that he was a sinner. (d) God's answer out of the whirlwind, and the epiphany of his majesty and greatness. (e) The repentance of Job and the restoration of his prosperity and his family. Then follow the lessons: (a) The certainty of our trial in being separated from the things which provide worldly happiness. Can we stand the test as Job did? (b) God is to be obeyed and trusted, rather than explained and discussed. "Though he slay me, yet will I trust in him." (c) If we know so little about God and his ways in the physical universe, it must not be strange that there are mysteries too deep for us in his providence. (d) The purpose of life is probationary, to try our souls and to produce spiritual and moral qualities. This is what is called "the end of the Lord." (e) In the hour of trial remember Job. Remember "the end of the Lord," that he is very pitiful and of tender mercy.

The character of Pilate is a subject that never wanes in interest. When we preach on the subject of "Conscience," there is no character who fits it better than Pilate. What a story, what a battleground of conscience Pilate was! How determined he was, as Peter said, to set Jesus free, and how he tried every way to escape the guilt of condemning Jesus to be crucified. In telling the story of Pilate and his battle, the following truths can be brought out: (a) The suddenness, the unexpectedness, with which the crises of the soul arise. When Pilate took his seat on the judgment bench that morning, little could he have known what that day was to mean for him. (b) The good there is in even a wicked and cruel man like Pilate. He recognized at once the innocence and the majesty of Christ. Christ spoke to the better man in Pilate. (c) The dream of Pilate's wife. Pilate's own impressions about Jesus, confirmed by his private examination of him, were now confirmed by the mysterious dream of his wife. This was, as it were, a truce offered to his soul. (d) The surrender of Pilate. The shout from the mob, "If thou let this man go, thou art not Caesar's friend," brought the battle to an end. Pilate counted his present world of more value than the future. (e) The final and irrevocable verdict on Jesus: "What I have written I have written." That truth was the title he put upon the cross. But in a larger sense it was the verdict of condemnation and rejection. Everyone eventually writes the final verdict of his soul concerning Christ.

In dealing with these engrossing characters, such as Balaam, Jacob wrestling with the angel, Judas, and Pilate, it is well for the preacher to avoid the discussion of things which are difficult, if not altogether impossible, to explain. For example, in the story of

Balaam, upon the second visit of the ambassadors of Balak, the Lord told him to go with the men. But afterward the Lord was angry because he went, and an angel with a drawn sword stopped Balaam on the way. Then when he said, "I have sinned," and was ready to turn back, the angel told him to go on. There is no need of perplexing a congregation with a discussion of these apparent contradictions. Drive home the great lessons of Balaam's character, such as avarice, spiritual aspiration without the willingness to pay the price, and tampering with conscience. In preaching on Judas, it is just as well to pass over the difficult question whether Jesus knew that he was a traitor from the beginning, and yet chose him for the apostolic band.

One of the greatest characters of the Bible, declared to be the greatest in the world up to his time, is John the Baptist. If Jesus were speaking of John today, I have no doubt that he would still say of him, "Among them that are born of women there hath not risen a greater than John the Baptist." Here are the great things about John for the preacher to mark and declare: (a) The greatness of his conviction. There has never been a great life or a great witness without a great conviction back of it. (b) The greatness of his humility—like the moss upon the rocks in the forest. "He must increase, but I must decrease." (c) The greatness of his courage. John's denunciation of the scribes and Pharisees and of Herod and Herodias, when he might have made himself a popular leader. (d) The greatness of his message, "Behold the Lamb of God, which taketh away the sin of the world." There is all the gospel. That declared takes in all else. That left out leaves out everything.

Some of the most helpful and interesting biographical sermons can be preached on Bible characters about which just one fact may be known. Such themes give the preacher opportunity to construct a biography—in a sensible way, of course—out of a sanctified imagination. The greatest epitaph of the Bible is that pronounced by Jesus upon one of the Christian disciples in the city of Pergamos, "Antipas was my faithful martyr, who was slain among you, where Satan dwelleth." (Rev. 2:13.) That is all we are told about Antipas. But what a chord of imagination that brief record strikes. It is easy for us to imagine the conversion of Antipas in that wicked city: (a) A believer in Christ, in spite of a hostile and most wicked environment. (b) A faithful Christian, in spite of worldly and financial loss. Probably he was a man who held a high post in the pagan world. (c) A faithful Christian, in spite of ridicule and reproach. (d) A faithful Christian, in spite of the fact that he was one of very few in the midst of the great city. (e) A faithful Christian, in the face of persecution and the threat of death. Such was Antipas. Of all the thousands and tens of thousands who have followed Christ since he arose from the dead, Antipas is the one signaled out for glorious and immortal mention by Christ. "Antipas was my faithful martyr, who was slain among you, where Satan dwelleth."

143

V

PREACHING WITHOUT NOTES

WHEN MOSES WAS CALLED TO SPEAK BEFORE PHARAOH and command him to let Israel go, he drew back from that high assignment:

And Moses said . . . , O my Lord, I am not eloquent . . . but I am slow of speech, and of a slow tongue. . . . And the anger of the Lord was kindled against Moses, and he said, Is not Aaron the Levite thy brother? I know that he can speak well. . . . And he shall be thy spokesman unto the people.

In every field of human endeavor the man who can "speak well" has a great opportunity and a great influence. In law, in statesmanship, in politics, in military affairs, and increasingly in the business world, the man who can speak well exerts great power. But the preacher stands in the most influential place of all. Edward Irving, one of the kings of the pulpit, used to speak of the "Royal Order of Preaching." It is indeed a "Royal Order." Ours is the imperial task to speak to the imperial though sin-scarred soul of man, to uplift Christ and his cross, as God's ambassador to show sinners the path of virtue, to paint the splendors of the heavenly life. For such an imperial task we

144

may well covet the highest gifts, and for the fulfillment of this task we ought to be willing to subject ourselves to the severest labor and discipline.

Every consecrated man in the ministry strives to preach in the most effective way. As the years go by, we think less about preaching a "good" sermon, and more about preaching a sermon that will *do* good. The question is: What method of preaching is likely to do the most good? The finest arrow that can be made is nothing without the steady eye which directs it, and the keenest wrought Toledo blade is nothing without the arm that wields it.

At the outset let me say that there have been great and effective preachers of every style—reading, memoriter, with notes, and without notes. But in season and out of season, year after year, and to the average congregation, there can be no question that the sermon that does the most good is the sermon which is preached without notes.

Here at the beginning let me sound a note of warning. Let no one choose this method because he thinks thus to deliver himself from the bondage of pen or memory. By no means! Preaching without notes is by all odds the hardest way, both as to preparation and as to delivery. Whitefield, who was one of the pioneers in preaching without notes, was attacked on this ground by professors at Harvard who declared that no strong argument could be handled convincingly without a manuscript. Whitefield answered: "Indeed, gentlemen, I love to study and delight to meditate.

Preaching without notes costs as much, if not more, close and solitary thought, as well as confidence in God, than with notes." There is no doubt about that. It takes more out of a man, both in the preparation and in the preaching. Let no minister choose this method for any reason except that experience proves it to be the most effective.

In 1720 the General Assembly of the Church of Scotland declared that the reading of sermons was "displeasing to God's people and caused no small obstruction to spiritual consolation." As a general principle, this still holds true. The reading of a sermon may entertain, instruct, and even move a congregation. It may be used by the Holy Spirit to save a soul from death. But it is never preaching in the highest sense. Who could picture Jesus reading the Sermon on the Mount, or the parable of the good Samaritan, or the story of the lost son, or of the lost sheep? Who could think of him reading his sevenfold denunciation of the scribes and Pharisees? Who could think of Paul reading his sermon to the philosophers on Mars' Hill, or even turning aside to consult notes in his hand as he spoke? Who could think of Paul standing on the seashore at Miletus and reading to the elders of the church at Ephesus his beautiful valedictory address? Who could think of Peter on the Day of Pentecost pulling out a manuscript and reading the divine summons to repent and believe on the Lord Jesus Christ? Reading a sermon, however profitable and well done it may be, is not in reality preaching at all.

146

The radio has undoubtedly been a great blessing to thousands upon thousands of people, and it has been a spiritual blessing also to multitudes of souls. But radio speaking and radio preaching have exerted a baneful influence upon public speech. Nearly all radio speeches that people hear are read. The moment you turn on the radio, you can tell that the speaker is reading. This kind of speaking is often stimulating and helpful, but just as reading a sermon is not in the highest sense preaching, so reading a speech is not in the highest sense true oratory. The highest preaching and the highest oratory is the impact of one soul upon another in free and open address.

ADVANTAGES OF PREACHING WITHOUT NOTES

One great advantage of preaching without notes is the power of a direct appeal. Richard Storrs, the famous Brooklyn preacher of the last quarter of the nineteenth century, studied law at Boston before he entered the ministry. He listened to Rufus Choate and other noted members of the Boston bar, and observed that all these men never read their arguments when they spoke before the bench or to the jury. When he became a preacher this convinced him of the advantage of preaching without notes. If, when a man's temporal interests are at stake, his lawyer would never think of pleading his case with the jury by reading his arguments, then why should a preacher, who deals not with a man's temporal and material interest, but with his immortal soul?

147

Preaching without notes gives an earnestness to the preacher which is hardly possible otherwise, and it is earnestness that counts. That is the true eloquence. Dr. James McCosh, the famous president of Princeton, was a brother-in-law of Thomas Guthrie, the great Scottish preacher, and for a time was minister in a neighboring parish in Scotland. He speaks of the crowds that would flock to hear Guthrie when he came to hold services on a summer evening, and thus comments on the earnest and emotional note in his preaching: "Some hard men thought that his discourses were not very logical; some finical men and women regarded his Forfarshire accent as very broad, and his illustrations rather vivid; but they all went to hear him because they got their hearts warmed." One morning someone asked Lord Cockburn where he was going to church, and he answered, "Oh, I am going to hae a greet [cry] with Guthrie." Guthrie warmed men's hearts. That was the secret of his success. And no preacher can warm men's hearts with a manuscript. Think of the things no one would try to say with a written address or with notes. In a time of disaster or danger who would read his call for help? Who would attempt to stir men's hearts before going into battle by reading them a discourse? And who would read the expression of his love to the woman of his choice?

Another advantage of preaching without notes is the full play it gives to the preacher's personality. Think of a man's face, especially his eyes. Men used to speak of the meteorlike flash of Calhoun's eye when he was delivering his great speeches in the Senate. The eye on a written page can never be as effective as the eye fixed on a human countenance. "Iron sharpeneth iron; so a man sharpeneth the countenance of his friend." A preacher may have little or much personality, but certainly, when he gets into the pulpit he needs to use all that he has.

Again, the man who preaches without notes may avail himself of a quick welling up and outbreak of imagination, something that had not occurred to him at all when he was pondering the sermon. Or he may be able to make quick and effective use of some happening or particular environment. Edward Irving was once preaching in Perth on the coming of the Son of Man. While he was engaged in unfolding his subject, suddenly, from out of a dark cloud which had obscured the church and the congregation, there blazed forth a flash of lightning, and then the crash of thunder, followed by a deep silence. Irving paused for a moment, and then out of the stillness and gloom, with great solemnity, pronounced these words, "For as the lightning cometh out of the east, and shineth even unto the west; so shall also the coming of the Son of man be." Had Irving been reading a manuscript, that powerful use of his text would have been impossible. On one occasion Whitefield was preaching in the fields, and a man climbed a tree near his pulpit to mock at the preacher. But instead of being discomfited by this, Whitefield turned to him and, likening him to

149

Zacchaeus, invited him to come down out of the tree and receive Christ into his soul.

One of the most serious handicaps to the preacher is monotony of speech and utterance. It is true that even the preacher without notes can frequently be monotonous, especially if he is a memoriter preacher, recalling verbatim what he has written and prepared. The only difference between reading a manuscript and reproducing a sermon verbatim from memory is that in one case you read it from a piece of paper and in the other from the back of the mind. But the chances for monotony are much less if a man is preaching without notes. In conversation the voice is rarely monotonous, and if a preacher feels what he is saying and speaks without notes, he is much less likely to fall into the singsong monotony which mars the effect of many a good sermon. Finney, the great revival preacher of the nineteenth century, says, in his "Revival Lectures":

If a minister means to preach the gospel with effect, he must be sure not to be monotonous. If he preaches in a monotonous way, he will preach the people to sleep. Any monotonous sound, great or small, if continued, disposes people to sleep. The Falls of Niagara, the roaring of the ocean, or any sound ever so great or small, has this effect naturally on the nervous system.

One more advantage of preaching without notes is that when it is done after experience, and with a degree of liberty of utterance, the preacher himself gets a joy out of preaching that he can have in no other way. When a preacher gets joy out of his own preaching, it is pretty certain that the congregation will also. Few preachers got such joy out of their preaching as Henry Ward Beecher. He said that many preachers were chained to their sermon, laboriously dragging it after them, but he, like Elijah, rode triumphantly heavenward in the chariot of his sermon. He said that frequently his sermons would leave him in such an exalted state of mind that he would not get over it for several days—"I feel it all day Sunday and Monday, and there is not an organ in the world that makes music so grand for me as I feel in such supreme hours and moments."

DRAWBACKS AND DANGERS

One of the dangers and drawbacks is the temptation to a lazy man to substitute glibness of speech for premeditated truth and the beaten oil of the sanctuary. Such a man will run a wire with molasses on it down into a barrel of illustrations, select some that appeal to him, apply them to some current event, and thus in short order prepare a sermon, which, for a little season, may deceive even the elect. But time, that inexorable exposer, is sure to reveal his shallowness and his laziness.

Occasionally the man who preaches without notes may fall victim to some disconcerting incident while he is in the pulpit. Even a hostile face in the congregation may divert his mind or confuse his thought. A young preacher once came to Spurgeon in great distress. He complained that as soon as he commenced to preach one of his deacons who sat in the front pew would stop his ears with his fingers and lower his head. It thoroughly upset him. What was he to do? Spurgeon broke the minister's tension with his answer, "I would pray the Lord to send a fly to light on the end of his nose."

On one occasion I was preaching the ordination sermon for a friend in a Philadelphia church. My subject was "The Miracles of the Gospels and Their Witness to Christ." At the end I wished to summarize the sermon by summoning before the pulpit an imaginary company of those whom Christ had healed—blind Bartimaeus, the daughter of Jairus, the Gadarene possessed of the devils, the woman with the issue, and Lazarus. I said: "I see standing in the back of the church a considerable company of people. I would like to say a particular word to you. There is plenty of room here in these front seats, and if you will come forward I can address myself to you." To my amazement and temporary discomfiture, quite a few people who were sitting in the back pews made their way down the aisle with much noise and took seats in front. It took no little skillful maneuvering on my part to address them as Bartimaeus and Lazarus and the other men and women whom Christ had healed. Nevertheless, that very event which almost wrecked the sermon also demonstrated the compelling power of the spoken and direct appeal. Who in all the world could have got those people to leave their seats and come down the aisle to the front pews if he had been reading a manuscript?

Sometimes when the minister who preaches without notes has finished, he will be dismayed to discover that he has omitted some of his most important and effective passages. Sometimes he will realize that before he finishes his sermon. But, as a rule, it is unwise and dangerous to go into reverse and try to salvage those lost treasures. It is much better to keep them for another Sunday.

There are also times when, because of some burden on the preacher's mind or heart, or perhaps because of physical fatigue, his mind does not kindle, is not candescent. As he labors along, it is like whipping a tired horse. No doubt there will be many times when the preacher would have done better had he, under such circumstances read his sermon. But if a man has set himself to preach without notes, he ought never— even under trying conditions—to fall away from it and go back to a manuscript. It is far better to fail now and then without a manuscript than to run the risk of being bound by one. Despite some of these drawbacks which I have noted, the advantages of preaching without notes far outweigh the disadvantages.

THE SECRET OF PREACHING WITHOUT NOTES

A great preacher and philosopher once said that genius means God and a dungeon. I suppose he meant that there must first of all be the gift of God, and then hard labor and solitude. Of all sermons, those which are preached without notes require the severest labor beforehand.

One of the secrets of effective free preaching without notes is a careful outline and a logical development of the subject. Like a cathedral, a man, a ship, or a horse, a good sermon is a unity where part fits into part. Thomas Guthrie, who wrote all his sermons in the morning before eight o'clock, had a blank page alongside each written page. If he found that any passage he had written was difficult to memorize, he rightly concluded that it was obscure, and he recast it until it became luminous and easy to recall. "Be clear when thou judgest," said the psalmist. To every preacher ought to be given this admonition: "Be clear when thou preachest; for thine own sake and for the sake of the people who hear thee."

I myself like the old plan of a simple outline with few divisions, including a statement at the beginning pointing where the preacher intends to go and how he intends to get there. Suppose one is preaching on such a theme as "The Precious Blood of Christ." (I Pet. 1: 19.) His purpose is to state, according to the Scriptures, what the blood of Christ accomplishes. There are four effects of the blood of Christ as taught in the New Testament: it justifies, it redeems, it cleanses, and it reconciles. It is not difficult to recall the points and heads of a sermon like that. When I speak of preaching without notes, I do not mean taking a sheet into the pulpit with the heads and a few subheads of the sermon jotted down. I mean *having no notes whatever.* Those heads and subheads can be written on your mind just as indelibly as on a piece of paper. In the old rhetoric book which I used in California I remember a statement to the effect that the object of speech is to convey thought. Not a bad definition. If the preacher has definite thoughts to convey, there is no reason why he should not be able to convey them in direct speech, and not through the written page.

One of the most effective preachers of the nineteenth century—often called "the preacher's preacher" —was Frederick W. Robertson, of Brighton. But he was much more than a preacher's preacher. He was decidedly a "people's preacher." His sermons show the advantage of outline, and he emphasized the clarity of outline as an aid to memory: "Without method, memory is useless. . . . It simply depends upon correct arrangement. The words and the sentences are left to the moment. The thoughts methodized beforehand and the words rightly arranged will place themselves. But upon the truthfulness of the arrangement all depends." Quoting another, he says, "If you are feeling sure of your subject, you may be quite sure your discourse will go off well. The hard work is done before you get into the pulpit. To the well-prepared man the work is easy there."

Another secret of free and easy preaching without notes is the minister's physical fitness. When body and mind are tired, it is hard to preach in any fashion, and doubly hard to preach without notes. Therefore the importance of the care of the body. It has been

155

well said that if the preacher does not sleep over his sermon Saturday night, the congregation will sleep over it on Sunday morning. The real test and trial for him who preaches without notes is the second, or Sunday night sermon. In the morning a man has a sort of electrical energy which carries him along, but at the evening service he must draw on his reserve of physical energy. Hence the importance of being thoroughly prepared for the evening service. The preacher should always make it a point to get that sermon out of the way first, and have it firmly fixed in his mind. Nothing is more wearing on a preacher than to begin to labor over his evening discourse on Sunday afternoon, before his mind has relaxed from the strain of the morning sermon.

With all this, of course, goes the preacher's spiritual fitness. "No man," said Phillips Brooks, one of the kings of the American pulpit, "can firmly succeed in the ministry who cannot make men believe that he is pure and devoted." The life that the preacher lives during the week will either augment his power in the pulpit and give him joy in the proclamation of his message, or diminish his power. The recollection of unworthy words or unworthy deeds will track him up into the pulpit and take the ring out of his voice and the joy out of his message. John Milton said that a poet ought to be a poem himself. Likewise the preacher ought to be a sermon himself. In a letter to the students at Harvard and Yale, who were to carry on the great movement he had started, Whitefield wrote this sentence, which every minister would do well to bear in mind: "Henceforward, therefore, I hope you will enter into your studies, not to get a parish, nor to be polite preachers, but to be great saints."

THE USE OF MEMORY

There are those who say that preaching without notes is possible only for certain types of men—those who have a good memory. But I question if there is the great difference in men's memories that we sometimes think. Educators hold that a man can be trained to do almost anything. If you make up your mind to do it, you can write on the tablets of your mind just as clearly as on a piece of paper, and you can read it again with your mind's eye just as easily as with your physical eye. Nothing works until it is tried. Your memory will not serve you unless you give it a trial and put your faith in it.

What about a mental blackout? What is a man to do when everything goes from him and he has no manuscript to fall back on? Such an awkward situation gives the preacher an opportunity to practice faith as well as to preach it. There is a well-known minister who once told me how he received his definite Christian conviction and was afterward led into the ministry. In the country church where he worshiped, the preacher was a dull fellow who would often forget parts of his sermon. Whenever he did so, he fell back on the Psalms and would quote them. It was those quotations from the Psalms which more than anything else

157

impressed this young man and led his footsteps toward the ministry. It is a good thing for the preacher to have passages from the Psalms as well as other portions of the Scriptures on the tip of his tongue. No matter what the subject of the sermon, great passages from the Scriptures will strengthen and adorn it. As one is quoting those passages, it is quite likely that he will recover the lost thread of his discourse.

It is well to remember that what the preacher may suppose to be a dreadful pause, as he stands for a moment on the brink of nothingness, will not seem nearly so long to the congregation. A young Scottish preacher in the midst of his sermon happened to see the renowned Dr. Chalmers in his congregation, and was so discomfited that for a moment he lost himself and had to pause for what seemed to him a very long time before he could go on. The next day, walking on the street, he saw Chalmers approaching; and, conscious of what seemed to him his failure on the previous day, he felt no little embarrassment when the great preacher stopped to talk with him. But Chalmers commended his sermon and the manner of delivery, especially the effective pause; adding: "Young man, cultivate the pause! Cultivate the pause!"

What about quotations? To be used effectively these must of course be memorized. But the average sermon has far too many quotations. The greatest preachers —such as Chalmers, Guthrie, and Beecher—rarely quoted. In all Beecher's sermons I recall just one poetical quotation, and that a magnificent one, Charles

Wesley's great hymn on Jacob wrestling with the angel:

> Come, O thou Traveler unknown,
>   Whom still I hold, but cannot see:
> My company before is gone,
>   And I am left alone with thee:
> With thee all night I mean to stay,
> And wrestle till the break of day.
>
> I need not tell thee who I am,
>   My sin and misery declare;
> Thyself hast called me by my name—
>   Look on thy hands, and read it there:
> But who, I ask thee, who art thou?
> Tell me thy name, and tell me now.
>
> Yield to me now, for I am weak,
>   But confident in self-despair;
> Speak to my heart, in blessing speak;
>   Be conquered by my instant prayer:
> Speak, or thou never hence shalt move,
> And tell me if thy name be Love.
>
> 'Tis Love! 'tis love! thou diedest for me!
>   I hear thy whisper in my heart;
> The morning breaks, the shadows flee;
>   Pure, universal Love thou art:
> To me, to all, thy mercies move;
> Thy nature and thy name is Love.

Spurgeon quoted stanzas from familiar hymns, but not much else. When poetry is quoted, it should be something both lucid and luminous, with an appeal to the heart of man. As for prose quotations, the average congregation can read these for themselves. They prefer to hear what the preacher has to say for himself. The overfrequent use of poetical quotations has a tendency to make the preacher a mere declaimer, rather than a proclaimer of the everlasting gospel.

When I was a senior in the theological seminary at Princeton, Dr. David James Burrell, then at the zenith of his distinguished ministry at the Marble Collegiate Church, New York, came to Princeton Monday nights to hear the seniors preach and criticize their sermons. He urged and inspired the men to preach without notes. And no doubt there are many free preachers in the pulpit today who owe him a debt of gratitude. I recall my own experience when I went out at the end of my junior year in the seminary to a picturesque little village in Wisconsin. I had my first sermons well in hand, but I had copious notes on the pulpit Bible. I did not refer to the notes, but the fact that they were there chained me, as it were, to the pulpit. After a few Sundays had passed, I abandoned the manuscript altogether and launched out into the great deep of preaching without notes. Since then I have never preached either with a manuscript or with any notes whatsoever in the pulpit.

THE EXPERIENCE OF FREE PREACHERS

When Henry Ward Beecher held his first pastorate in Indiana, he wrote out in full all his sermons in the

160

exalted style of Robert South. But when he came to deliver these sermons in the pulpit, he found that mind and body suffered, as from the recoil of a heavy piece of ordnance. Finding that he had little joy and freedom in delivering these sermons, he would sometimes abandon altogether the sermon upon which he had been working most of the week, and would preach on a theme which had taken possession of him on Saturday—"to get rid of it." He says that he made many vows with himself, endeavoring to break the habit, but finally gave up and prepared his sermons mostly on Sunday morning and on Sunday afternoon. But it is important to remember what he says in connection with this, that his preaching was accompanied by regular study and continual observation: "I do not believe that I ever met a man on the street that I did not get from him some element for a sermon. I never see anything in nature which does not work toward that for which I give the strength of my life. The material for my sermons is all the time following me and storming up around me." There were always, he said, a dozen or more topics lying loose in his mind during the week. After breakfast on Sunday he would go into his study as a man goes into his orchard and feels among the apples to find the ripest and the best. He would then select the theme which seemed the ripest, choose a text, and analyze the subject. Often he would still be writing the introduction when the church bell rang. Then he would snatch up the manuscript and hurry to the church. When the time for the sermon came, with his notes lying before him on the open Bible, he would read in a rather quiet voice the first few pages and then, throwing his manuscript aside as he was caught up by the inspiration of the hour, would launch forth on one of his great discourses.

Charles Spurgeon followed much the same method. When Theodore Cuyler visited Spurgeon late one Saturday afternoon, that preacher with the marvelous voice told him that he had not yet selected a text for the next day's sermon, but that presently he would go down into the garden, choose a text for the morning and evening, and then outline the morning sermon. Sunday afternoon he would make an outline of the evening sermon. Spurgeon never composed a sentence in advance, and spent little time laying out the plan of the sermon.

Thomas Guthrie, on the other hand, carefully wrote out his sermons and committed them to memory. But his delivery was so natural that it seemed like an extemporary address. Usually he had before him a single sheet of paper containing the sermon headings. Bishop Matthew Simpson, who stirred the multitudes and lifted congregations out of their seats, determined from the beginning to be an extemporaneous preacher in the real sense of the word. All that he did was to make a brief outline on one sheet of paper.

Thomas De Witt Talmage, who drew large congregations, never used a manuscript. In his early days he preached with his manuscript before him and generally read the sermon. On the first Sabbath in his first church at Belleville, New Jersey, he had his sermon at his side on one of the great horsehair sofas which used to adorn American pulpits. To his dismay, the sermon slipped through the opening in the back of the sofa and fell behind it. While the congregation was singing the second hymn, he had to get down on his hands and knees and retrieve his manuscript. This embarrassing incident raised doubts in his mind about manuscript preaching. But it took one more incident to convince him. On the first day that gas was used in the church, he planned to read the introduction of his sermon, and then "let go" as an extemporaneous preacher. But as he drew near the end of his manuscript, his courage began to fail him, and he prayed earnestly that the lights would go out. His prayer was answered just as he reached the end of the written manuscript, and the church was plunged in darkness. He dismissed the congregation, saying, "It is impossible to proceed." But when he went home to his manse and began to think it over, he felt it was humiliating that a man with a message from God should have to depend upon gas meters and a paper mill. It was after this episode that he began to preach without notes and became so distinguished an example of the extemporaneous preacher.

It goes without saying that Whitefield, the great field preacher, preached without notes. No man could have held the multitudes that he drew if he had read his sermon. No man who reads a manuscript can be

163

heard by great multitudes like the man who lifts up his head and pours out the message from his heart. Whitefield's least effective sermons were those which he wrote in his early ministry. Now and then —but not often—he would go apart with those three still good friends, Adam Clarke, Matthew Henry, and Cruden's *Concordance* and meditate for a season. But he always claimed that the best preparation for preaching was preaching itself. There is much in that. Most of us do not preach often enough, and we have a tendency to develop a stilted, artificial manner when we do preach. Whitefield expressed great regret when his failing health put him on what he called "short allowance"—once every day and three times on Sunday. Benjamin Franklin, who delighted to hear Whitefield, thought that his written sermons and the published sermons gave no intimation of the preacher's great power, and that his most effective sermons were those which he had preached over and over again, and from which he deleted the ineffective passages. On many occasions Whitefield held great multitudes spellbound without any preparation at all. "Sometimes," he says, "when twenty thousand people were before me I had not in my apprehension a word to say, either to God or to them. But I was never totally deserted, and was frequently, for to deny it would be lying against God, so assisted that I knew by happy experience what our Lord meant by saying, 'Out of his belly shall flow rivers of living water.'"

One of the most effective free preachers of the last

generation was Francis L. Patton, president of Princeton University, and later president of Princeton
Theological Seminary. Dr. Patton gave lectures in
Christian ethics at the seminary. On those occasions
he read from manuscripts which he had evidently
written years before. My recollection is that nothing
could have been duller than those lectures. But in the
pulpit he was a different man. There he had no manuscript and no notes. It was a great experience for
those of us who were looking forward to the ministry
to see Dr. Patton take a text, open it up in his logical,
analytical, yet always human and sometimes poetic
manner, advancing in orderly procession from proposition to proposition. Now and then he quoted a line or
two of poetry, generally, as I recall, from Tennyson's
In Memoriam. If a man is going to preach doctrinal
sermons, the way to make them real and vital to a
congregation is to preach them as Dr. Patton did,
without notes.

The year after I left the seminary I spent my vaca-
tion in Bermuda. In those times the whole population
came down to see the steamer arrive. As my ship came
slowly in, I spied Dr. Patton standing near the end
of the dock. I went up to my old professor and made
myself known, and he was kind enough to invite me
to preach for him in St. George's Church, Warwick,
where he was preaching for the summer. I was wise
enough to decline the invitation, but on Sunday evening I went to hear him preach. The gallery was filled
with Negroes; the white people sat below. But Dr. Pat-

ton talked to them all just as if he were preaching at Princeton. His text was, "Let us hear the conclusion of the whole matter," and he "went every where preaching the word." At length he got on the theme of the future life; and, wishing to illustrate the greater light on that subject which shines in the New Testament, he quoted the twenty-third psalm, calling it the high-water mark of the Old Testament faith in immortality. "Yea, though I walk through the valley of the shadow of death, I will fear no evil: for thou art with me." Lifting up his arm and marking an imaginary line on the stone pillar above his head, he said, "That is the high-water mark of Old Testament faith in immortality—willing to go, but wanting to stay." Then he quoted Paul's words, "For I am in a strait betwixt two, having a desire to depart, and to be with Christ; which is far better: nevertheless to abide in the flesh is more needful for you." Then, lifting his hand still higher on the stone pillar, he said, "That is the high-water mark of New Testament faith in immortality—willing to stay, but wanting to go."

One of the pioneers in free preaching in America, and one of the most powerful of all preachers, was Charles G. Finney. Some of his contemporaries in the ministry found his manner of preaching without a manuscript startling, even shocking. Early in his career he was asked unexpectedly by the presbytery in session at Evans Mills, New York, to preach them a sermon. He suspected it was a trap to catch him without preparation and expose his shortcomings. Nevertheless he responded to the invitation. But instead of going into the swallow's nest pulpit, high up on the pillar, he amazed the presbytery by standing free and clear on the lower platform and talking to them as man to man. His legal training undoubtedly inclined him toward this method of preaching. He advocated illustration and reiteration in preaching, saying that when a successful advocate addresses a jury, he repeats over and over again the main points which he wishes to impress on their minds.

One of Finney's most famous sermons was that on the Atonement—"One mediator between God and men, the man Christ Jesus." (I Tim. 2:5.) Dr. E. A. Park, then a student at Andover Seminary, heard him preach that sermon in the village church in 1831. Half a century after hearing it Dr. Park said:

His sermon was just one hundred minutes long. It held the unremitting attention of his hearers, even those who had opposed his interference with our seminary exercises. It abounded with sterling arguments and with startling transitions. It was too earnest to be called theatrical, but in the best sense of the word it was *dramatic*. Some of his rhetorical utterances are indescribable. I will allude to one of them, but I know that my allusion to it will give no adequate idea of it.

Finney was illustrating the folly of men who expect to be saved on the ground of justice, who think that they may perhaps be punished after death, but that when they have endured all their deserved penalties

167

they will be admitted to heaven. He was appealing to the uniform testimony of the Bible that the men who are saved at all are saved by grace. They are pardoned, their heaven consists in glorifying the vicarious atonement by which their sins were washed away. He was describing the jar which the songs of the saints would receive if any intruder should claim that he had already endured the penalty of the divine law.

The tones of the preacher then became sweet and musical as he repeated the words of the "Ten thousand times ten thousands, and thousands of thousands; saying with a great voice, Worthy is the Lamb that hath been slain to receive the power, and riches, and wisdom, and might, and honor, and glory, and blessing." No sooner had he uttered the word "blessing" than he started back, turned his face from the mass of the audience before him, fixed his glaring eyes upon the gallery, at his right hand, and gave all the signs of a man who was frightened by a sudden interruption of the divine worship. With a stentorian voice he cried out: "What is that I see? What means that rabble-rout of men coming up here? Hark! Hear them shout! Hear their words: 'Thanks to hell fire, we have served out our time. Thanks! Thanks! WE HAVE SERVED OUT OUR TIME. THANKS TO HELL FIRE!'" Then the preacher turned his face from the side gallery, looked again upon the mass of the audience, and after a lengthened pause, during which a fearful stillness pervaded the house, he said in gentle tones: "Is this the spirit of the saints? Is this the music of the upper world? 'And every created thing which is in heaven, and on the earth, and

168

under the earth, and on the sea, and all things that are in them, heard I saying, Unto him that sitteth on the throne, and unto the Lamb, be the blessing, and the honor, and the glory, and the dominion, forever and ever. And the four living creatures said, Amen.' "

During this dramatic scene five or six men were sitting on a board which had been extemporaneously brought into the aisle and extended from one chair to another. I was sitting with them. The board actually shook beneath us. Every one of the men was trembling with excitement. The power of the whole sermon was compressed into that vehement utterance. It is more than fifty-eight years since I listened to that discourse. I remember it well. I can recall the impression of it as distinctly as I could a half century ago; but if every word of it were on the printed page, it would not be the identical sermon of the living preacher.

That is a splendid illustration of a great and stirring pulpit appeal, one which would have been utterly impossible had the preacher been using a manuscript.

HELPFUL TOPICS

The preacher who is going to preach for the first time without notes would do well to start with Bible biography or the Bible stories. These themes give him something easy to remember. There is always a certain advantage in preaching on the great characters and the great narratives of the Bible. And, of course, any story is always better told than read. When one tells a story from the Bible, or bases a story on the

169

life of a Bible character, he will find plenty of illustrations in the story itself.

The subject of deepest interest to man is man himself. Sermons which are based on life and life's experiences not only hold a congregation but lend themselves to free presentation on the part of the preacher without need of a manuscript. Then there are the great doctrines. As we have seen in the case of a great doctrinal preacher, Dr. Francis L. Patton, the best way to present these majestic truths is in free extemporary speech. That gives them a reality and vitality not possible to draw from a manuscript.

If a man has been accustomed to preach by manuscript and wants to try preaching without one, he will meet with difficulties at first, and may even frequently fail. But he must make up his mind to be undaunted by failure. If he believes that this is the best way to preach, then he ought to be willing to labor and sacrifice himself to the utmost to master the art. I remember once seeing an exhibition by some Russian acrobats in a Moscow park. When it was over, I said to my friend who was with me, also a minister, "If we prepared ourselves as thoroughly for our work in the pulpit as those acrobats have prepared themselves for this exhibition, we would be better preachers."

The preacher must be ready to sacrifice a reputation of profundity or scholarship for effectiveness and greater influence and good as a preacher. Some time ago I read a sermon by a popular preacher of the Southwest on the text: "They that be with us are more than they that be with them," the words of Elisha to his servant who was frightened by the Syrian hosts which beleaguered Dothan. Compared with some of the sermons which appear in high-class ecclesiastical and homiletical magazines, this was no sermon at all. But comparing those polished sermons with this one on Elisha, I realized that those carefully written discourses, despite their literary allusiveness, could never have held or stirred a great audience as much as this simple sermon on the resources of the Christian faith, in which the preacher went through the Bible and cited instance after instance to show how God is always with his people. This printed sermon held and interested me. It must have stirred the people who heard it.

But whatever method the preacher decides to employ, let him give himself wholly to it. Let him preach with the conviction that it makes the greatest difference in the world whether he does his work well. Let him speak to the souls of men, realizing that they are created by God and fitted to hear the word of God, and let him expect that the soul will respond to the voice of God. Let the preacher remember that he is speaking to souls who are at the parting of the ways, and for whom this may be like John's great "tenth hour," when he who hears may see and find the Lord.

And always let him preach God's message with a warm heart. This was the prayer that was so often upon the lips of George Whitefield, that great hunter of souls—"O Lord, grant me a warm heart!" When the preacher preaches with a warm heart, a living faith, and a clean life, whether he preaches from a pulpit in a great city or in some quiet village, or in a church on a hilltop beneath the shadow of the oaks and the hickories, or out on the frontier, then, as God said to Ezekiel, whether they will hear or whether they will forbear, men shall "know that there hath been a prophet among them."

God of the prophets! Bless the prophets' sons:
Elijah's mantle o'er Elisha cast.

VI

THE MINISTER'S OCCUPATION

MIDNIGHT ON THE MEDITERRANEAN, THE WIND HOWL-
ing and the sea raging. The night black as ink. The
great waves crashing over the ship. The ship surging up
now to heaven, now sinking to the depths. The decks
swept clear of every movable article. Masts gone, sails
gone, rudder gone. The ship's company at their wits'
end, and all the pagans on their knees, imploring such
gods as they know to deliver them out of destruction.
But fast asleep in the hold of the vessel lies the one man
who ought not to have been able to sleep that night—
the runaway prophet. Guilt can sleep as well as innocence. Peter slept calmly and peacefully that night
between the two soldiers to whom he was chained
in the prison of Herod with the death sentence upon
him. But guilty Jonah sleeps just as soundly in the
hold of that storm-driven vessel. Finding him asleep
there, the captain of the ship awakens him, amazed
that he can sleep when all others are gripped by terror,
and says to him, "What meanest thou, O sleeper?
arise, call upon thy God, if so be that God will think
upon us, that we perish not."

The seamen have come to the conclusion that the
storm which has broken over them and the death which

is threatening them must be due to the misconduct of someone who is on board the vessel. They are nearer the truth than they think. It was Achan's sin which caused the defeat and overthrow of Joshua's army before the walls of Ai. Here it is the sin of Jonah that has brought the storm upon the ship. There is profound moral truth in that! Who knows how much injury to the work of a church may be done by the unworthy life of a single member!

On the ship the seamen gather about the bowl which holds the lots, and by the dim light of the ship's swinging lantern you can see the anxiety on each one's countenance as his pricking conscience brings to life again some transgression of the past. This one is thinking of a child he kidnapped at Alexandria, that one of a merchant he robbed and threw over the sea wall at Tyre, and this one of a girl he seduced at Thessalonica. Each man recalls the "plague of his own heart." But each breathes a sigh of relief when his hand draws a blank. "And the lot fell upon Jonah."

When the lot falls upon Jonah, the seamen say to him, "Tell us, we pray thee, for whose cause this evil is upon us; and whence comest thou? what is thy country? and what people art thou?" That question—"what is thine occupation?—brings Jonah to himself. He remembers who and what he is. He says to the seamen, "I am an Hebrew; and I fear the Lord, the God of heaven, which hath made the sea and the dry land." He tells them how he has fled from the presence of the Lord. That question, "What is thine occupation?" is the turning point in Jonah's history.

Jonah is the greatest preacher in the history of the world. Of no other preacher is it recorded that he brought a whole city and a kingdom to its knees in repentance. Yet this greatest of preachers made a poor start. He fled from his commission to preach to Nineveh. A simple question by the sailors on the storm-driven vessel restored Jonah to himself and his great work.

"What is thine occupation?" This is a suitable question to be addressed to young men in the theological seminary preparing for the work of the ministry. It is also a suitable question for the minister to ask himself from time to time, in any hour of discouragement or hurt, in any time of lowered standards, or in any moment of temptation. "What is thine occupation?"

A DIVINE OCCUPATION

The minister's occupation is appointed of God, not of man. The current tendency is to secularize the ministry, both its message and its office, as if the work of the minister were just the same as that of a teacher, a physician, a scientist, or an artist, only with a slightly different accent. This has done the church no good. It has not honored the gospel, nor strengthened the church, nor brought men into the ministry. The minister's occupation is a divine occupation. "He gave some, apostles; and some, prophets; and some, evangelists; and some, pastors and teachers; for the perfecting of the saints, for the work of the ministry, for

175

the edifying of the body of Christ." Thus the ministry is a divine occupation, and the pulpit is, as our fathers used to speak of it, "the sacred desk." Because the office of the minister is of divine origin, and because we have received of God, not of man, this ministry of reconciliation, the pulpit has stood secure through all the ages, in spite of the faults and limitations of those who have stood in it. It will continue to stand, and continue to speak, until time shall be no more.

THE OCCUPATION OF A GOOD MAN

At the head of the holy procession of mankind always walks the good man. Of the greatest pastor of the Old Testament, Elisha, it was said by that Shunammite woman at whose home he was entertained frequently, and where at length a prophet's chamber was built for him, "Behold now, I perceive that this is an holy man of God, which passeth by us continually." There is the ideal for the minister's character and industry—"an holy man of God, which passeth by us continually." A minister is expected to be a good man. Except for a few poisoned and embittered minds, most people will take it for granted that he is a good man, a godly man. But the minister himself must never take that for granted. The thing for him to remember is what Christ said to Peter, "Satan hath desired to have you, that he may sift you as wheat." Satan desires to sift the minister above all other men, sift him out of his industry, his prayer, his watching, his zeal, his convictions, and his enthusiasm.

176

In the prophecy of Zechariah we have an account of the ordination of the high priest Joshua. Before the throne of God, Joshua stood in the presence of the angel of Jehovah. At his right hand, ready to accuse him, stood Satan. Joshua was clothed in filthy garments. At the angel's command the garments were taken from him, and a clean robe was put upon him, signifying his purification and forgiveness. Then the angel repeated the Lord's message, "If thou wilt walk in my ways, and if thou wilt keep my charge, then thou shalt also judge my house, and shalt also keep my courts, and I will give thee places to walk among these that stand by." As Satan stood by the side of Joshua, ready to accuse him and, if possible, prevent his consecration, so at the right hand of every young minister who is about to commence his work stands the Adversary, ready to accuse him, to soil his consecration, sift him of his character, steal away his enthusiasm, and quench the light of his faith.

Thus it is that the minister must always take heed to himself, must always preach to himself, and pray to himself, and fight for himself, lest it be true of him, as Cardinal Newman wrote:

> Thou to wax fierce
>   In the cause of the Lord,
> To threat and to pierce
>   With the heavenly sword!
>
> .   .   .   .   .   .
>
> Thou warnest and smitest!
>   Yet Christ must atone

For a soul that thou slightest—
Thine own.

The motto for every earnest minister ought to be
that of the great Minister, the great Shepherd himself, who said, "For their sakes I sanctify myself."
The better the man, the better the preacher. When he
kneels by the bed of the dying or when he mounts
the pulpit stairs, then every self-denial he has made,
every Christian forbearance he has shown, every resistance to sin and temptation, will come back to him
to strengthen his arm and give conviction to his voice.
Likewise every evasion of duty, every indulgence of
self, every compromise with evil, every unworthy
thought, word, or deed, will be there at the head of
the pulpit stairs to meet the minister on Sunday morning, to take the light from his eye, the power from his
blow, the ring from his voice, and the joy from his
heart. It is a great thing for the preacher when "they
of thine own house"—the words, thoughts, and deeds
of his own life—are on his side and not against him.

A MAN WITH A MESSAGE FROM GOD

In one of the tragic and dramatic scenes of the Old
Testament a Hebrew patriot appears suddenly in the
presence of the tyrant king of Moab and says to him,
"I have a message from God unto thee." What he
had was a terrible message of retribution and assassi-
nation. But what that left-handed deliverer of Israel
said to the tyrant of Moab before he smote him ought

to be true of every minister of the word of God, "I have a message from God unto thee."

It was early morning in the country beyond the river Jordan. David stood in front of the fortress at Mahanaim to review his troops as they marched into battle against the rebellious Absalom. The earth shook with the tread of thousands of armed men as they passed before David, the bugles blowing, the pennants streaming in the morning air. One division was under Abishai, a second under Ittai, a third under Joab. As each division marched before David it was halted for a moment while David spoke this message to each commander, "Deal gently for my sake with the young man, even with Absalom." Then the troops marched on, leaving behind them a cloud of dust and the faint echo of their trumpets.

All day David paced up and down before the fortress, refusing meat and drink and conversation with his officers, for his heart was in the great battle raging in the wood of Ephraim. Absalom's raw recruits proved no match for the veteran soldiers of Joab, and Absalom himself, caught by the luxuriant tresses of his hair in the branches of an oak as he was fleeing from the battlefield, was transfixed by three darts from the hand of Joab. His body was cut down and cast into a pit. As Joab's soldiers marched past, each one, muttering an execration, flung a stone down upon the body, until a great heap covered the mutilated corpse of David's rebel but beloved son. That was his tomb, instead of the beautiful mausoleum and pillar which Absalom had reared for himself in the king's dale, where he had expected to be buried with royal honors. The morning sun saluted the beauty of that tomb, the evening sun gilded it with gold, and the moon bathed it with ethereal light. But it was a tomb without a body, a monument without a man. Not there, but in the stone-covered pit in the forest lay Absalom's body.

After the battle Ahimaaz came to Joab and asked the privilege and honor of bearing tidings to the king. Joab refused to let him run, and instead sent Cushi, the Ethiopian. But Ahimaaz came a second time to Joab and again begged permission. Joab said to him, "Thou hast no tidings"; but, yielding to the youth's insistence, he let him run. He was a faster runner than Cushi, and soon overtook and passed him. From the top of the fortress wall the watchman could see him coming far in the distance, and reported to David that a runner was approaching. When he learned that it was Ahimaaz, David's heart was glad, and he said, "He is a good man, and cometh with good tidings." Presently Ahimaaz came up to the king, and, saluting him, cried, "Blessed be the Lord thy God, which hath delivered up the men that lifted up their hand against my lord the king." But that was not what the king was thinking about. That was not what he wanted to know. What he was thinking about, what he wanted to know, was what had happened to Absalom. So he said to the runner, "Is the young man Absalom safe?" And Ahimaaz answered, "I saw a great tumult, but I knew not what it was." Then the king said to him,

"Turn aside, and stand here." Ahimaaz had no tidings.

Soon the Cushite runner came panting to David and, saluting, said, "Tidings, my lord the king: for the Lord hath avenged thee this day of all them that rose up against thee." Then came the question on David's heart, "Is the young man Absalom safe?" And Cushi answered, "The enemies of my lord the king, and all that rise against thee to do thee hurt, be as that young man is." When David heard that, he wrapped his mantle about him and, climbing the stone stairway to the chamber over the gate, wept. And as he went, he moaned, "O my son, Absalom, my son, my son, Absalom! would God I had died for thee, O Absalom, my son, my son!" There was a man with a message.

There you have the difference between the preacher with a message and the preacher without a message. Ahimaaz was faster than the Cushite runner and, no doubt, had better form; but when he stood before the king, he had nothing to tell. There are preachers who have better form, better diction, better education than others, but who, when they arrive in the pulpit, have no message to deliver. Asked about the meaning of life, all they can say is, "I saw a great tumult. Life is just a tumult, 'full of sound and fury, signifying nothing.' I saw a great tumult—much joy and much sorrow—but what it meant I knew not."

Such a preacher has no message because he has no authority. Joab had given no tidings to Ahimaaz. The preacher without the message speaks without authority. He cannot track the sinner down and say,

181

"Thou art the man!" He has no message of atonement for sin, no ringing word of hope for the world or for the individual. In *Mark Rutherford's Autobiography* the author tells how he and his friend McKay were once passing St. Paul's Cathedral, London, and McKay said that he had once thought that if only he could stand in a pulpit like St. Paul's and there speak to his fellow men, he could bring a message which would regenerate mankind. But after a little reflection he concluded that all he would have to say would be, "Dear friends, I know no more than you. We had better go home." All that the world can say, and does say, to such a preacher is what David said to that runner out of the wood of Ephraim: "Turn aside, and stand here."

But look now at the preacher with a message. Cushi was not as fast as Ahimaaz, nor was his form as good. He was far outdistanced, although he had a long start. But when he arrived at the fortress in the wilderness, he had the message which broke the king's heart and sent him mourning to the chamber over the gate. The true preacher has tidings because he knows the meaning of life. He knows that life is more than a tumult in the wood. He knows what the "chief end of man" is. He knows that man is called, as Paul said, to "glory and honor and immortality, eternal life." He does not come with his own message, or speak out of his own authority. He speaks, not with the human dogmatism, but with the divine dogmatism—"Thus saith the Lord!"

When George Whitefield was getting the people of Edinburgh out of their beds at five o'clock in the morning to hear his preaching, a man on his way to the tabernacle met David Hume, the Scottish philosopher and skeptic. Surprised at seeing him on his way to hear Whitefield, the man said, "I thought you did not believe in the gospel?" Hume replied, "I don't, but he does!"

The preacher with a message knows the "plague of his own heart," and of every other man's heart. He can speak the judgment of God upon sin. But he can declare also the message of God's forgiving love, the message which brought the doxologies leaping from the lips of the apostles and the saints, as they wondered that God should have commended his love to men who were sinners. He can bring the message that Christ died, the Just for the unjust, the message of a forgivness so wonderful that it can turn a blood-stained and guilty murderer and robber on the cross into a fit companion for the Redeemer as he enters paradise. And now even the greatest angel of heaven dare not stand before that thief and say to him, "I accuse thee!"

The true preacher has a message of hope for the individual and for the world. In answer to the inquiry of man's anxious heart, "Watchman, what of the night?" all that this preacher—this watchman on the wall without a message—can say is, "The morning cometh, also the night." That is all that the scholar, the historian, the scientist, the philosopher can say,

"The morning cometh; but also, and always, the night." Tranquility, and then storm. Peace, and then war. Hope, and then agony. Life, and then death. Night and its shadows blotting out the mountains of mankind's expectations. But the preacher with a message can say more than that. He can say: "The morning cometh, also the night." But also, and finally, and forever, the morning! The morning without a cloud. The morning when the sun shall go no more down by day. The morning when the ransomed of the Lord shall return, and come to Zion with songs and everlasting joy upon their heads, and shall obtain joy and gladness, and sorrow and sighing shall flee away. The morning when the last enemy shall be put under Christ's feet, and God shall be all and in all. The morning when the morning stars which sang over creation shall sing once again over man's redemption. The morning when the seventh angel shall sound, and great voices shall be heard in heaven saying, "The kingdoms of this world are become the kingdoms of our Lord, and of his Christ; and he shall reign for ever and ever."

This is the message—and this the occupation—of the minister. Great is the responsibility of the minister to that message. It is, as Paul called it, "the glorious gospel of the blessed God, which was committed to my trust." There are other beautiful, tender, and sacred trusts—the trust a sick man puts in his doctor, the trust a congregation puts in its minister, the trust a friend reposes in a friend, the trust a bride

184

puts in her husband, the trust a little child puts in his father and mother. All these are sacred trusts. But none of them is comparable to that trust which God reposes in the minister whom he has set apart to preach the glorious gospel of the blessed God. Because we shall give an account of what we have said from the pulpit, let us be sure that what we say is that sacred message with which we have been entrusted

Sometimes by one tragic transgression the minister will forsake and betray his occupation, but more often the decline is gradual. When the king of Egypt came to Jerusalem and captured and sacked the city, he stripped the walls of Solomon's beautiful House in the Wood of its golden shields and carried them to Egypt with him to adorn the temples of Isis and Osiris. Instead of mustering his army and marching after the invaders and winning back those stolen shields of gold at the point of the sword, Rehoboam, king of Israel, made shields of brass and hung them on the walls of the House of Wood. Is not that the tragedy which overtakes many a minister? He becomes satisfied with a second best, or even a third best. He sinks into secularity, sloth, or indifference. Compare the shields that hang on the walls of his study, on the walls of his church, on the walls of the house of his own soul, with the shields of gold which once hung there, and lo, they have become shields of brass.

What, then, is thine occupation? May that question which brought Jonah to himself and back to his mission as a prophet, that night on the storm-tossed ship in the waters of the Mediterranean, speak to all our souls, rebuke us when we need to be rebuked, shame us when we need to be shamed, and renew and inspire our devotion to that glorious gospel of the blessed God with which we have been entrusted.